Action Trumps Everything

Action Trumps EVERYTHING

Creating What You Want
in an Uncertain World

CHARLES F. KIEFER
LEONARD A. SCHLESINGER

with PAUL B. BROWN

Black Ink Press

2010

Black Ink Press
20 Screenhouse Lane
Duxbury, MA 02332
www.actiontrumpseverything.com

ISBN: 978-0-9831319-1-5

Cover and interior design by Rebecca Saraceno
Typefaces: PMN Caecilia with Avenir
Cover image: © thinkstockphotos.com.

This book is manufactured in the United States of America.

To Saras D. Sarasvathy, whose research and insights remind us how we can all think entrepreneurially.

A NOTE FROM THE AUTHORS

This is very much a work in progress.

Since we really do believe Action Trumps Everything, it was important for us to get these ideas out into the world as quickly as possible to learn what people think of them, and to see how they could be improved.

That's where you come in.

After you have read the book, please go to ActionTrumpsEverything.com and give us your thoughts. Yes, of course, we want to know what you liked, and what you didn't. But we also want to know how you have applied these ideas in your life and business.

We will take all that information, synthesize it, and create Version Two of the book. That, too, is in keeping with what we believe is the best way to navigate in an uncertain world: Act. Learn. Repeat.

Our guarantee

Our promise to you:

If you follow the handful of principles in the following pages, whatever you want will come closer within reach.

Signed:
Charles F. Kiefer, Leonard A. Schlesinger,
and Paul B. Brown

Postscript: You will note we are not guaranteeing success in whatever you do (although following these principles should give you a more fulfilling and therefore successful life).

But we are guaranteeing that if you fail, you will fail quickly and cheaply, and that (as you will see) is almost as good.

Table of Contents

An introduction to where we are heading

or how we came to find a way to navigate effectively in an uncertain world. This is all you need to know about **Action Trumps Everything** in a single place. It will take you just six minutes of reading time to figure out if what we propose is right for you. And if it is not, you might like the drawings.

Since this chapter is supposed to be a guide to the pages ahead—so you can understand where we are going and decide whether you want to come along—maybe the best place to begin is by explaining why we wanted to write this book in the first place.

Initially, we headed down this road out of curiosity. There were two things we didn't understand as we tried to reach our professional and personal goals (and our guess is these two things, from time to time, have bothered you as well).

Curiosity #1 deals with how we were taught to think.

Growing up, we liked school. We have come to think of the process our teachers taught us to follow as Prediction Reasoning—from now on we are just going to refer to it as Prediction—a way of thinking based on the assumption that the future is going to be pretty much like the past.

Demographics are one simple example of how Prediction works. You can calculate with a high degree of confidence what the world population will be in 2050 because you know a lot of things. Here are just four:

1. You know how many people are alive today: about 6.8 billion.

2. You know how those people are distributed by age, i.e., you know how many teenagers there are, how many people over 65, etc.

3. That means you know how many people are in their 20s and 30s, the time when most people decide to have children.

4. And you know recent trends in population growth—it's slowing as people worldwide are, on the whole, deciding to have fewer kids.

Studying all this data—and much, much more—you can, as the United Nations did recently, say with a high degree of certainty that come the year 2050 there will be 8.9 billion people on the planet. And armed with that data you can also make a number of fairly accurate estimates of certain things, such as how many diapers will have to be produced; how many gallons of water those 8.9 billion people will drink each day; and how much America will need to pay out in Social Security benefits when we reach the midpoint of this century.

As a society as a whole, we have gotten really good at Prediction. To support this kind of thinking, we have developed great analytic tools (statistics, probability, computer simulations, etc.). These tools are—as a scientist would write—logically bounded and complete. That's a fancy way of saying they yield the correct solutions, and the same solutions, every time.

Math is great. There are right and wrong answers and it is

consistent. You can teach it. It allows us to do wondrous things. You want to send a rocket to the moon and land at a specific spot (even though the moon will be in orbit, i.e., moving, while the rocket is in space)? No problem. Prediction allows us to do that. Need to estimate with a level of certainty how many sports cars will be sold during a recession? Prediction can help you do that as well.

Because it works so well in these kinds of situations—and countless others you can think of—we (like you) became accustomed to using Prediction all the time. Like anything, if you do something over and over, it becomes a habit. Your view of the world becomes conditioned.

And yet . . .

Not everything can be foreseen (and thus predicted). Want to know if the cute guy across the hall is going to ask you out? Sorry, Prediction can't help. Desperately need to know if the town council is going to go for your idea of turning Main Street into a pedestrian mall before you spend your nights and weekends working on the project? Prediction is of little use.

> You can't predict when faced with
> fundamental uncertainty. You need an
> alternative. Luckily, you already have it.
> Hint: It is the reasoning you used as a toddler.

If you want a reasonable guess as to whether a polo shirt that is selling well in Cincinnati will also be popular in Sacramento, Prediction is great. Half the equation is known. The current product and market exist. We can project, based on experience, how well that polo shirt will sell once it is introduced elsewhere. But want to know if an unfamiliar product—say a polo shirt with a three-quarter length sleeve—will work in a virgin market? Sorry. While there is some data that might be informative, Prediction leaves you pretty at. It just can't help you. Nor is it any help with predicting whether your totally new nonprofit/public service/community project idea will find acceptance.

So that was curiosity number one. Faced with an unknown universe—and it sure seems to us that as the world becomes more complex, there are more unknowns out there—the Prediction reasoning we were brought up with was increasingly letting us down.

Curiosity #2 deals with people who don't act the way all the research says they do.

If you ever took an economics course, you might think people are rational and that they make the best possible decisions for themselves, their family, and friends.

Decades of research—and everyday experience—says that is just silly. People make terrible, or at least seemingly sub-optimal, decisions all the time, whether we are talking about investing, job choices, or love. They don't make the best decisions, they—in the words of Herbert Simon, who won the Nobel Prize for this insight—"satisfice."

That's a wonderful word he invented which combines satisfy and suffice. And that is what people do almost all the time, they satisfice. You know if you hit 1,000 golf shots every day for the rest of your life, you could improve your handicap from a 13 to a 10. But who has time? So, you live with the fact that you will probably shoot 85, not 82, on a regular basis. You know you should be doing a better job preparing for retirement, and yet you never seem to do much about it.

Conversely, it doesn't make any "rational" sense to collect every Superman figurine ever made, or to learn everything there is to know about the Eastern goldfinch if you are not an ornithologist, yet people do this sort of thing all the time. Human beings act to fulfill desires, not to achieve an intellectual ideal of optimization.

It seemed the whole concept of "desire" was lacking from the decision-making literature as well.

So there we were. We were frustrated because we just didn't know the best way to make a decision when the future is unknowable. And frustrated because we didn't truly understand where desire fit into the decision-making process, although we knew it was important.

Enter our friend Saras Sarasvathy.

If it works for them . . .

Saras, now a tenured professor at the University of Virginia's Darden School of Business, earned her Ph.D. at Carnegie Mellon, where Herbert Simon was her faculty advisor. One of her specialties is entrepreneurship. Early in her work, she made a fascinating discovery, one that ran counter to the conventional wisdom about people who start companies.

When people write about entrepreneurs, they invariably focus on their behavior: what Howard Schultz or Michael Dell did in building their companies. If you take that approach you might conclude that every single entrepreneur is unique, and so there is little to be learned from studying them; you would have to be Howard Schultz to start Starbucks and Michael Dell to start Dell.

Conversely, Saras, who is the author of *Effectuation: Elements of Entrepreneurial Expertise* (Edward Elgar Publishing), focused on how the people we term "serial entrepreneurs" think. And there she found amazing similarities in how they reasoned, approached obstacles, and took advantage of opportunities. Yes, of course, there were variations. But the basic approach, as she understood it, was always the same.

In the face of an unknown future, they acted. More specifically:

1. They take a small (smart) step forward;

2. Pause to see what they learned by doing so; and

3. Incorporate that learning into what they do next.

This process of: Act. Learn. Repeat. continues until they are happy with the result, or they decide that they don't want to (or can't afford to) continue.

We became tremendously excited after we read Saras' research and put our own (Act. Learn. Repeat.) spin on it. We tested our ideas with colleagues and held more than a dozen seminars where we invited smart, skeptical people to challenge our conclusions. They helped us refine and clarify our thinking, but our central findings only grew stronger as they told us about their experiences, which reinforced what we had learned. It looked like we might have a way to resolve our two major curiosities. Clearly, many entrepreneurs spend a great part of their day dealing with the unknown—they are selling products and services that never existed before and there is no way to predict with certainty whether they will be successful. And obviously desire is central to everything they do. (Even someone who has never dreamed of starting a company knows you really, really have to want to do it, given how challenging the task is.)

So, we began looking at Saras' research and wondered if the way entrepreneurs think would work for the rest of us.

Before moving on, there are a couple of things to note about that statement.

First, while we will use some business examples throughout the book, we will use even more that come from everyday life. This is not a business book in the traditional sense.

Second, when we set off to see if the way entrepreneurs think would work for the rest of us, we weren't looking to replace Prediction.

There were two reasons we weren't.

- As we have seen, Prediction works really well when the future can realistically be expected to be similar to the past.

- Second, Saras' work—which we will cite throughout—shows entrepreneurs use Prediction effectively in the situations where it works well, i.e., in the places where it is logical to assume that the future will be a lot like what has come before.

So, we were NOT looking to replace Prediction. Rather, we wanted to know whether the logic entrepreneurs employ when they face the unknown—we came to think of it as CreAction, a word we shaped that combines "creation" and "action"—would work for the rest of us when we face a situation where the future is essentially unknowable. In other words, could CreAction be used to complement Prediction in the everyday situations ("can I convince the town to add a bicycle lane downtown?"; "will anyone buy what I have to sell, if I start a company?"; "would I be happy chucking it all and joining Teach for America?") that we frequently find ourselves in?

> In studying successful entrepreneurs, researchers found a common logic that allows them to deal with situations where the future is not predictable. It turns out, what works for entrepreneurs will work for the rest of us.

Lo and behold, we found that what works for entrepreneurs will work for the rest of us—in business settings and elsewhere. **There is *indeed* a way of thinking you can use to complement the kind of reasoning we all have been taught—an additional way of thinking that can help you deal with high levels of uncertainty no matter what kind of situation you face.**

Here's what we are talking about

So, what exactly is this CreAction that we are going to be talking about in the pages ahead? Well, here's a starting point: It is based on *acting* and *creating* evidence, as *contrasted with thinking and analysis.*

Here's one way to think about this pivotal difference. A painter paints. Substituting thinking for painting doesn't work. If all you do is think, you don't end up with a picture. Thinking is often a part of creating, but without action nothing is created. This is true even for very intellectual, cerebral fields. For a task to be considered creating, you must publish, teach, or whatever. Meditating in a cave with no action is not creating.

How does CreAction play out in practice? How does it help us deal with uncertainty? The process goes like this:

- Find/think of something you want. You only need sufficient desire to get started. ("I really want to start a restaurant, but I haven't a clue if I will ever be able to open one.")

- Take stock of the resources you have at hand right now that can help you achieve it: what you know. Who you know. And anything else that's available. ("I know a great chef, and if I beg all my family and friends to back me, I might have enough money to open a place.")

- Using those resources, take a smart step toward achieving your goal, i.e., bring your current reality closer to what you want. ("Let me see what the rents are like at potential locations.")

- Pause to re ect on what you have learned from taking that step. Every time you act, reality changes. Sometimes it gets nearer to what you want ("I should be able to afford something just outside of downtown"); sometimes what you want changes ("It looks likes there are an awful lot of Italian restaurants nearby. We are going to have to rethink our menu."). You always learn something. So after you act, ask: Did those actions get you closer to your goal? ("Yes. It looks like I will be able to open a restaurant.") Do you need additional resources to draw even closer? ("Yes. I'll need to find another chef. The one I know can only do Italian.") Do you still want to obtain your objective? ("Yes.")

- Repeat until you have what you want (or you have decided you don't want it, and/or want something else instead).

In other words, when facing the unknown, **act your way into the future that you desire**. You don't think your way into it. Thinking does not change reality, nor does it necessarily lead to any learning. You can think all day about starting that restaurant, but beyond a certain point, it is not going to get you any closer to having one.

WHAT'S A SMART STEP?

In our description of how CreAction works, we said people take "smart steps" toward what they want. So, what's a smart step?
There are four parts:

Act quickly with what is at hand.

Determine what you can *afford* to pay to play and what you *want* to pay to play. (These can be different. You may be able to afford to spend $50,000 on a new idea, but are only willing to invest $10,000.) In other words, before setting out, figure out how much you are willing to risk—in terms of time, money, and reputation.

Bring other people along. Having many people involved in whatever you are trying to do allows you to both gain more assets to draw on—the additional assets belong to the people you have brought with you—and to spread out the risk.

Build off the unexpected. Invariably, as you move toward your goal, you will encounter things that you simply had no way of knowing were going to be there. You can turn those problems or obstacles into assets. (Don't worry. We will show you how.)

Repeat these four steps until:

a) You don't want to continue. (You changed your mind; something else is more appealing.) Or

b) You exceed your affordable loss. Or

c) You prove to yourself it can't be done.

As a child, everything was unknown or uncertain, so you started learning through action. You'd make a sound and something happened (your mother responded). You tried to pull the cat's tail (and got scratched). Over time we all learned to use Prediction and got very good at it. But in that process we have become, we believe, overly dependent on "thinking our way into better actions."

Moreover, as we have seen, all that thinking doesn't help you much in the face of the unknown. It works great when you can predict. It doesn't when you can't.

What we will be advocating in the pages ahead amounts to the recovery of a skill we all had a long time ago: the ability to act your way into better thinking. We are NOT saying this replaces Prediction. It complements it. When Prediction makes sense, predict. When it doesn't, try CreAction. As you try to deal with a new situation you will invariably bounce back and forth between the two. And that is exactly right.

In fact, we have a term for the process of using both forms of reasoning simultaneously: Entrepreneurial Thought and Action. That's our phrase for using BOTH Prediction and CreAction to solve a problem or create something new.

THE INTERPLAY BETWEEN
PREDICTION AND CREACTION

Invariably, as you try to create something new, you will move back and forth between Prediction and CreAction. (The combined use of both makes up what we call Entrepreneurial Thought and Action.)

Each CreAction step begins with a predictive element. You take a step because you think you know what the outcome will be. Then you compare what happens with what you thought would happen.

That's all there is

There you have it. That's our book in a nutshell.

If you find the idea appealing, then in the pages ahead you will find a detailed description of how to use CreAction in all kinds of situations you may encounter at work and in your personal life.

If you don't, well, you still found out how the approach works. You took a small step into the unknown (learning about CreAction) and decided it's not for you. (And if you are still looking for something else to read, we hear the latest Stephen King thriller is very good.)

Incidentally, while there is tons of research that supports the ideas and arguments we will present, if you get something of value out of this book it will NOT be because we convinced you with these arguments. It will be because what we have to say resonates with what you already know. It will strike you as common sense.

To find out if it does, turn the page. The journey is about to begin for real.

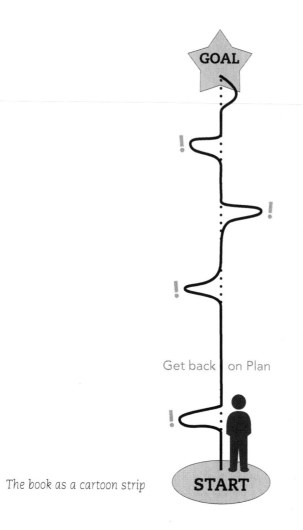

The book as a cartoon strip

In its purest form, Prediction is about forecasting, after extensive thought, what the future will be like, and setting a goal that will be the best possible outcome in that predicted future. Once the goal is set, you form a plan to achieve it, constantly correcting to stay on plan.

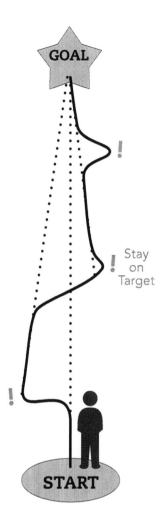

Of course, in most cases it is smart not to be wedded to the plan. You want to commit to the goal, not the plan, and when you are blown off course, re-plan just like a smart sailor would.

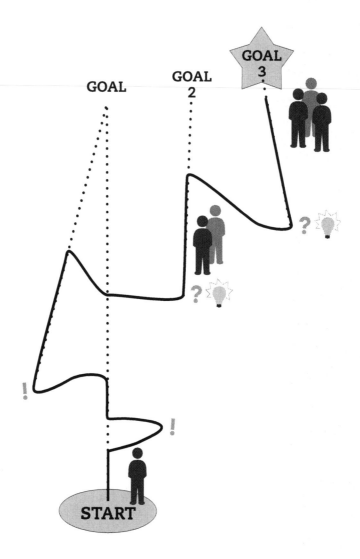

CreAction treats encountering obstacles and getting blown off course as positive and values opportunities to reconceive what is wanted.

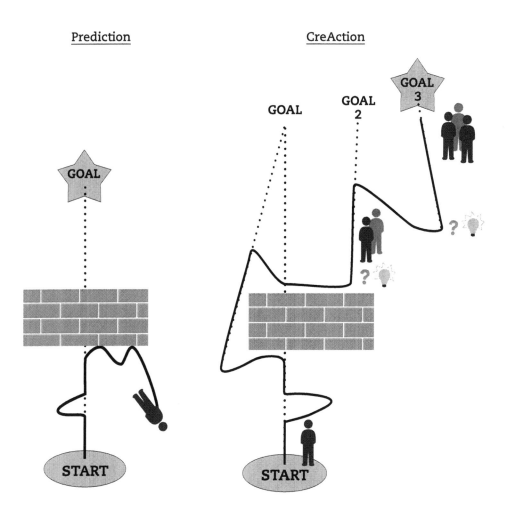

The difference between the two is obvious and acute when you encounter an obstacle that Prediction can't find a way around.

Entrepreneurial Thought

1

What's in this for you?

A funny thing happened on the way to creating this book: We followed our own advice and ended up with something far different (and we think far better) than what we set out to do, discovering a method that can improve your life. Here's an introduction to a new way of thinking: Creation reasoning, which we have captured in the word CreAction. It's a way of making decisions when the future is basically unpredictable.

This chapter is going to be about you. But to get there, we need to begin by talking about us.

This was supposed to be a traditional business book. We planned to write 50,000 words or so pointing out that entrepreneurs think differently from the rest of us. Not better. Just differently.

From there we were going to say that their different way of thinking works particularly well when you can't predict the future with any real accuracy.

The logical conclusion from those first two findings was clear. Since we are facing a business environment that seems to grow more unpredictable every day (as we write this in 2010, financial problems in Greece—Greece! the 27th largest economy in the world—threaten to take down GLOBAL financial markets), perhaps it is a good time to add the entrepreneurial lens to the way we view all business problems.

We weren't going to call for a wholesale revolution—like from now on you should ONLY think like an entrepreneur—we were just going to suggest that you may want to add that entrepreneurial lens to your decision-making tool kit.

Treating an uncertain world as if it were predictable only gets you into trouble.

To be honest, we felt pretty good about what we were going to do. That book (like this one) would be research-based. We had a catchy title: *Thinking Upside Down*; a major publisher was going to bring what we had to say to market, and we had even started to plan the clever bon mots we were going to drop when we were interviewed about all this. ("You know, Charlie/Barbara/Regis/Oprah, when financial problems in a tiny country like Greece cause global stock markets to swoon, maybe it is time to rethink everything.") So life was good and we started merrily on our way to creating *Thinking Upside Down* . . . and then the whole thing blew up in our faces.

Oops!

We know exactly the moment everything changed. We had finished the chapter that explains the difference between the way most of us think and the way successful serial entrepreneurs reason. And, as we mentioned, the difference is particularly stark.

Well before kindergarten, we've all been taught Prediction. *It is a pattern of thinking and acting that is based on the assumption that the future is going to behave in a way that is similar to the present and the immediate past.* It involves inferring and extrapolating, often using (sometimes very complex) analytic methods.

When we use Prediction in business (or business classes), we begin with both a predetermined goal—we want to create a new widget, or a unique service—and a given set of means. ("Here are the resources we have—the money, people, time, etc.—to build that widget or create that service.")

Then with the goal and the resources clearly identified, we set off to identify the optimal—fastest, cheapest, most efficient—way to accomplish the objective. The make-vs.-buy decision in production, choosing the target with the highest potential return in marketing, and picking a portfolio with the lowest risk in finance are all examples of Prediction.

Serial entrepreneurs, as we said, go about things differently. Sure, they use Prediction some of the time, especially when their firms are up and running and they are dealing with the business problems every other executive faces. But they also employ what we call CreAction which boils down to this: The future may or may not be like the past, but you don't have to spend a lot of time wondering how the future will play out *if you plan to shape it.*

We were proud of the chapter. But when we finished it we realized two things:

1. Yes, our central insight that serial entrepreneurs reason differently from the rest of us was intriguing, but the world was not waiting to read yet another "think differently" book. There have been 8,617 of them as far as we can tell (and Apple has been telling the world to "think different" since it made the phrase the basis of its advertising slogan in 1997). Besides,

2. Thinking (differently or otherwise) is lovely *but absolutely nothing changes unless you act.*

And that's when the penny started to drop with all we had learned about entrepreneurs. **Yes, they think differently. But more importantly, their natural inclination is to put that thinking into immediate action to see if they are right.**

The image of entrepreneurs coming up with an idea, laboring feverishly to perfect it, and delivering their creation to the market full-born is often wrong. (See Chapter 2.) The much more typical path is that they come up with an idea. They take a small step toward implementation to see if anyone is interested, and if it looks like there is potential market acceptance, they take another step forward. If they don't get the reaction they want, they regroup. That regrouping could involve modifying the idea or moving onto something else if that small step convinced them the idea wasn't going to work; wasn't worth the bother; or simply is no longer of interest.

If you can't predict the future—and it seems increasingly you can't—action trumps thinking.

The process repeats until the entrepreneur succeeds, knows she is not going to, or decides there is another, more appealing opportunity to pursue.

The acting/learning (from the acting)/acting again (to learn some more) loop, as shown below,

is one of the key things that makes entrepreneurs so different— and so important to the rest of us. Traditionally, when you encounter an obstacle, you are told, "Don't be a wimp; redouble your efforts and power on through." Entrepreneurs take a different approach. Their approach to dealing with an unknown future is the reason we decided to change our plans about what we were going to write.

When the light bulb went on

What we realized, as we took a step back, is not only do serial entrepreneurs view the unforeseeable world differently, but how they go about tackling problems successfully *can be documented (as in the graphic above) and taught.* In other words, their methods are available to the rest of us.

Up until now, most studies of entrepreneurs have been somewhat problematic since they have focused on entrepreneurial behavior, which is indeed idiosyncratic; no two entrepreneurs do things exactly the same way. But we shouldn't have been looking only at their behavior. We should have been studying the thinking that leads to their behavior as well. And when Saras, and the faculty at Babson College, did, they saw that many successful entrepreneurs employed the learning-by-acting loop outlined in the graphic above as quickly as they could.

That was a huge "aha" moment for two reasons.

First, **in a world that is seemingly growing more unpredictable by the moment, you can neither think of everything—or even close to everything—nor map out the future with any real certainty. That means that Prediction alone is hopelessly incomplete today and may well become even more limiting tomorrow**.

Instead of *thinking* your way into a new way of acting, which is at the heart of using Prediction, you need *to act your way into a new way of thinking*. That's what entrepreneurs do when faced with the unknowable—and it is an approach that will work for you as well.

Second, **we came to understand that when you are faced with great uncertainty, this concept of act-your-way-into-thinking can work for you everywhere!!!**

A quick example will prove the point. Say you want to lose 30 pounds. You can think about losing the weight all you want, but if you keep your eating habits and exercise patterns exactly as they are, your weight will remain exactly where it is. Until you take action, nothing is going to change.

But what kind of action?

Well, in the Prediction world you would work out a plan. Maybe you would stop eating carbs, or follow the South Beach diet. You'd keep your eye on the prize—losing those 30 pounds—and invariably you would fail. The level of commitment required (high) and time frame (long) are just too much for most of us.

Entrepreneurs, and everyone else who employs CreAction, would attack the problem differently. They'd begin by taking what we have come to think of as a "smart step" (action) in the direction they want to go. It would not necessarily be overly aggressive ("I am only going to eat 500 calories a day") or focus on a big goal ("I am going to lose those 30 pounds in the next 60 days").

That smart step probably would be a statement like: "I want to lose one pound this week."

With that modest initial goal in mind, you are far more likely to eat a little bit less over the next seven days, and exercise a touch more. If at the end of the week you have found that you have indeed lost a pound (or perhaps more), you will say to yourself: "That wasn't so bad. Let's see if I can do it again next week." And if you fail, you try adding something else. ("Hmmm. If I keep exercising and eating less and have just one glass of wine with dinner instead of two, maybe that will work.")

And if that approach is successful, you try it again the following week—and keep repeating it until you have achieved your goal. You have broken down a big problem ("How the heck am I ever going to lose 30 pounds?") into a series of smart actions: losing a pound a week for 30 weeks.

Eureka!

You can see why we were so excited (and wanted to share what we had discovered with you). In writing this chapter we had inadvertently employed CreAction, the Creation reasoning used by successful entrepreneurs. We invested just a little bit of time and effort (we wrote a chapter); it didn't feel right, so we tried something else. We had inadvertently proven you can learn by acting—not only in a business context but just about everywhere else (writing a book, losing weight, whatever).

And so we scrapped our initial plan (although you will find a distilled version of our initial chapter on Prediction and CreAction within Chapter 3) and set off to write what you now hold in your hands. As the subtitle says, it is a guide for creating what you want in an uncertain world. While our focus is going to be employing CreAction in business (including starting new businesses) because these are the areas we know best, we will periodically sprinkle in other examples just to underscore that Entrepreneurial Thought and Action—the idea of using Prediction and CreAction together— works everywhere.

As you will see, we followed exactly the same logic entrepreneurs use in solving problems at the macro level—*thought* and *action*. You will understand exactly what to do and how to do it at each step.

Serial entrepreneurs have proven that this approach works.

We have proven it for ourselves, and we are interested in hearing how it works for you. Please write to us at ActionTrumpsEverything.com.

Takeaways from Chapter 1

1 | **You can't always get what you want** (by thinking). There are certain places where you *can* (and should) think your way into action. You probably can predict how many white T-shirts will be sold next year; how many soft drinks will be consumed; and how much a family needs to be earning to afford a weekly cleaning service. Armed with that fairly easy-to-determine information, you can create your plans accordingly. But where we don't have this level of certainty, the reasoning we have grown up with has serious limitations.

2 | **Don't get stuck by over-thinking.** Some problems—raising the GDP of developing nations, for example—seem so daunting that people freeze and do nothing. Accept for now that using CreAction could give us a tool for attacking things like this successfully (by breaking the huge problem into many, many tiny ones and *acting* to solve those small problems one at a time).

3 | **Try a new approach to just about everything.** The concept of a) determining what you want; b) taking a small (smart) step toward obtaining it; c) stopping and thinking about what you have learned; d) repeating works not only in business, but anywhere in life where you are faced with significant unpredictability.

CHAPTER

Everyone can do this

But before you can employ CreAction effectively, it helps to forget everything you ever learned about the people who employ it best—successful serial entrepreneurs. Otherwise, you are going to give yourself an awful headache.

"Whoa, whoa, whoa, and wait a second," we hear you cry. *"You mean to tell me that everyone can employ this new way of thinking, CreAction, where you act your way into learning and solving problems?"*

Absolutely.

"But I thought it was only entrepreneurs who thought this way?"

No. The understanding and underpinnings of this new approach are derived from the way serial entrepreneurs think when they are presented with a problem whose answer is simply unknowable using traditional logic, but it is NOT limited to them.

Oh, I see.

Oh. Wait. I don't.

We understand the potential confusion. Let's back up and try to clear away some of the problems that may be standing in the way of accepting that we all can use CreAction, a way of making decisions, when a) the future is basically unknowable and b) obstacles become assets you can use.

Ready? Here goes.

One confusing point is that it turns out we don't have a very good handle on the people who employ CreAction: entrepreneurs. We tend to think of them as a unique species. We do that, as we said in Chapter 1, because up until now we have looked primarily at their **behavior**, and that behavior is, in fact, idiosyncratic. No two entrepreneurs do things exactly the same way. And since each of them acts differently, if you concentrated only on their behavior, you would conclude only Bill Gates could have started Microsoft. And while this conclusion may well be right, it is of little value to you.

> Entrepreneurial behavior is often idiosyncratic. The thinking behind it is not. (It's based on common sense.)

But, it turns out that entrepreneur's idiosyncratic behavior stems from how they **think**. And if you study their thinking, you find commonalities. Once you do, you can understand how they employ CreAction, and you can use CreAction in your own way (which is really what the rest of the book is about).

That sounds simple enough. But getting there is complicated, because we need to overcome all the ingrained images we have when we hear the word "entrepreneur." To show what we are talking about, let's look at the story of H. Harriet Harrison.

SALSA QUEEN

Hard work, relentless determination, and the willingness to go it alone have allowed Harriet Harrison to carve out a new niche in one of the fastest growing food markets—and have made her extremely rich in the process

By Charles M. Wilheim

Before answering, H. (for Hillary) Harriet Harrison stole a quick look at the framed stock certificate hanging on the wall of her office just outside Bozeman, Montana.

"It *is* amazing, isn't it," she said. "For three years—1,058 days to be exact; I kept track—I lived on nothing but store-brand pasta with ketchup and salad, and now . . ."

She gestured out the window at her 400-acre horse ranch, the first thing she bought with some of the $90 million she received from selling 59% of her company, Yummy Olé: The American Salsa Co., to the public the month before.

Harrison, as entrepreneur-founders often do, had stood on the floor of the New York Stock Exchange (NYSE) and bought the first 100 shares of her initial public offering (IPO). It was those shares—now in an ornate gold frame with a tiny spotlight beaming down on it—that she kept glancing at every 20 seconds. It was as if she needed to constantly make sure she wasn't dreaming that she was suddenly worth almost $600 million (the money she received from the IPO, coupled with the value of her 41% of the company), and that those thousand arduous days were behind her.

"And those three years don't even include the six months I spent searching for the right idea," she added.

Harrison, now 34, was a brand manager at Kraft who had been itching to go out on her own, but she could never find a business concept that resonated with her. "Finally, I said 'to hell with financial security.' I quit Kraft and promised myself I would find the perfect idea for a company. I thought it would take me about a week."

Inspiration struck on day 174.

"I had been poring through analyst reports, talking to everyone I knew, constantly visiting supermarkets and restaurants, and reading all the trade pubs. The thing that kept jumping out at me was that salsa had replaced ketchup as the best-selling condiment in America. Salsa—you should excuse the pun—was hot. I knew there was an opportunity there. But I couldn't figure out what it was. I spent months beating my head against the wall, trying to figure out how I could get a piece of the market.

"I was so frustrated that one morning I called up a girlfriend and asked her to meet me for lunch, just so I could get away for awhile. And it was while I was at a T.G.I. Friday's, of all places, that the light bulb finally went on over my head."

And a little child shall lead her

"While I was waiting for Claire, I looked over at the next table. A young couple was trying to convince their toddler, strapped into a high chair, to eat something. He just wouldn't. I figured he didn't like the taste or texture of what they were offering.

"I didn't think much of it. I continued to look around the restaurant and skimmed another analyst report. For some reason, when I looked back at the table with the toddler, I glanced at what the father was having for lunch, and I saw he had small dish of salsa, not ketchup, to put on his burger. That's when it all came together.

"Yes, salsa is popular. But there had to be some portion of the market that, like the baby, didn't like the taste or texture. I thought, 'if you could make salsa more ketchup-like, you'd have a winner.'"

"I went home, looked up every salsa recipe I could find, and started working on ways to smooth out the texture and make the product a bit sweeter. It sounds simple, right? But I had to isolate every variable. Fresh tomatoes or canned? Regular sugar, natural sweeteners, or a sugar substitute? Could you go with fresh tomatoes and cooked vegetables?

"It turns out there were six key variables, and I tested every combination. That means I tried 720 different recipes. Even creating two of them a day, every day—weekends, holidays, no matter what—took me a full year.

"My friends kept telling me to let it go. Good enough would be good enough, and I could always refine things later. Or they suggested I simply sell my recipe to a solid company like Kraft and take a tiny royalty on every jar sold. And there were a bunch of folks I know who suggested I partner with someone like Heinz, which had the distribution and marketing in place. But all those things struck me as wrong. My name was going to be behind the product. I had to be the one who was satisfied. So, I continued creating two recipes a day, trying to find the right one."

When she finally got THE ONE, Harrison starting driving throughout the Helena area, where she was living at the time, trying to get supermarkets and restaurants to buy a jar or two.

"God, it was hard. I'd make six,

seven, eight sales calls a day, and get a sale one day out of two. Then I'd go home, make myself some pasta because it was quick and cheap, and then I'd create another batch of salsa and do it again the next day."

Eventually, she started making a sale a day and the people who bought it loved it, and reordered. Within six months she had hired a couple of part-time cooks to whip up the salsa, and within in a year she was subcontracting to a food manufacturer and hiring a national sales firm.

Still, "It wasn't until year three that I was actually able to take a salary. I know it sounds like a cliché, but I really did max out my credit cards, taking cash advances from one to pay another, and as the bills came due I borrowed from anyone I could. (Thanks Mom and Dad.)

"I remember the day exactly; it was June 16, a Thursday, when I thought I could afford to have something other than pasta for dinner. That was day 1,059 since I had started the company. I made myself a tuna fish salad and had two glasses from a $4 bottle of wine."

A year later, underwriters at Kidder Peabody would be buying her lobster and champagne in New York, as they tried to convince her (successfully as it turned out) to let them take her public. Eleven months later, Harrison was standing on the floor of the NYSE buying those 100 shares of Yummy Olé: The American Salsa Co. (ticker symbol: YOUS [pronounced "Yo, U.S." by traders]).

"And now you are here writing about my overnight success," Harrison says with a laugh. "Is there any advice I'd offer? Not really. I think my journey is pretty typical. But if I were forced to say something, I'd say: Stick to your guns; remain true to your vision— the salsa we sell today uses exactly the same recipe I came up with initially; remain passionate about your idea at all times; and keep plugging."

You probably found this article familiar. But it didn't appear in *Inc.*, or the late *Fortune Small Business*, or the small business section of *The Wall Street Journal*. And you'll neither find it in the archives of *Success*, *Entrepreneur*, "the up-and-comers" section of *Forbes*, nor, for that matter, in any other publication that devotes space on a regular basis to the doings of entrepreneurs.

We made it up.

And we did so for two reasons. First, we think it captures the slightly reverent tone the press takes in writing about successful entrepreneurs. It is as if they are describing a magic trick that they don't understand and so have trouble being skeptical.

Second, and far more important, just about every trait attributed to H. (for Hillary) Harriet Harrison is the conventional wisdom about how entrepreneurs act. And *much of that conventional wisdom is wrong*. We want to expose those myths for a couple of interrelated reasons:

- By picturing entrepreneurs as a unique heroic species, we end up believing that there are only a handful of people who can employ CreAction because it comes hardwired at birth. Nothing could be further from the truth. Not only can everyone employ the same approach to problem solving that entrepreneurs use, entrepreneurs' reasoning can be learned.

- As you will see, the methods that entrepreneurs actually employ as they go about creating draws on a form of reasoning that we were all born with. It is drummed out of us as we go through school. (In the pages ahead, we will show you how to get it back.)

But before we get into all that, we need to address those myths surrounding entrepreneurs, so that we can start on a level playing field when it comes to explaining how you can employ CreAction to improve your life.

It ain't necessarily so

The easiest way to talk about the myths surrounding entrepreneurs is to go back to the story of the imaginary "Salsa Queen." We will state the myth; show how Harrison embodied that fiction; and then describe what typically happens instead.

The myths tend to fall into three big categories.

Myth #1. Entrepreneurs concentrate on finding one perfect idea at a time. Harriet spent "six months . . . searching for the right idea." The reality is entrepreneurs—just like the rest of us—can come up with a dozen potentially commercial ideas before breakfast, if they set their minds to it. The problem isn't coming up with an idea. It is figuring out which one you want to spend your time on. (We will talk about this in Chapter 4.)

Related to the "perfect" idea is the belief that it comes into an entrepreneur's head fully formed. Remember when Harriet said she glanced at the salsa on the dad's plate, and then back to the baby, and "that's when it all came together"—she knew the world wanted a smoother, sweeter salsa?

We concede that this occurs every once in a while, just like love at first sight actually happens and there are some people who know at the age of three that they were born to be a doctor (and then they actually become one).

But the reality is in many cases, the potential entrepreneur only has a vague notion along the lines of: "Hmm, I have all these skills, I wonder what I can do with them?" or "I know all these people (or I can access all kinds of resources) and I wonder how I can use them to create a product or service that people want?"

The last part about this myth involves the belief that once the idea is fully formed, it is sacred. Even though once Harriet developed THE PERFECT SWEET SALSA FORMULA and it appeared never to change ("The salsa we sell today uses exactly the same recipe I came up with up initially"), she actually followed the serial entrepreneurs' recipe of always tweaking their ideas. Initially, Howard Shultz had Italian opera playing as background music at Starbucks. Michael Dell began his company by doing nothing more than assembling IBM personal computer knockoffs. The best entrepreneurs don't wait to see if their product or service is perfect, because they start searching to see if there is going to be market acceptance.

What follows from that is entrepreneurs who are exible when it comes to advertising and selling. Their marketing plans are not locked in stone, as the entrepreneurial myths would have you believe.

As you'll remember, during the start-up phase, people suggested to Harriet that she "simply sell my recipe to a solid company like Kraft and take a tiny royalty on every jar sold. And there were a bunch of folks I know who suggested I partner with someone like

Heinz, which had the distribution and marketing in place." Harriet ignored those ideas because she was convinced she KNEW how to build her brand. The best entrepreneurs are open to advice. They seek it out. They don't always take it, but they don't reject out of hand something that could help them.

Myth #2. It is the lone, obsessed genius who creates the new. As you will recall, Harriet tried 720 separate recipes in her kitchen until she was happy. And this is perhaps the most pervasive myth of all: that the entrepreneur comes up with the idea alone. Not true. Even the most celebrated inventors (like Thomas A. Edison) worked in conjunction with others. Harriet had no employees, and certainly no partners, during the early days. She cooked the salsa at night and went out and tried to sell it the next day. In reality, successful serial entrepreneurs often involve other people from the very beginning, believing that all of us together are smarter than any one of us.

And since they do work with others, they don't necessarily spend 24 hours a day every day, as Harriet did, developing their idea. Long before she was cooking by night and selling by day, she was trying out recipes. "Even creating two of them a day, every day—weekends, holidays, no matter what—took me a full year." While it is certainly true that some entrepreneurs work constantly, the same can be said about some doctors, lawyers, plumbers, and candlestick makers. How much time someone spends on the job is a personal decision.

Myth #3. They commit totally very early in the process. Remember how Harriet created a burning platform for herself? ("I said 'to hell with financial security.' I quit Kraft and promised myself I would find the perfect idea for a company"?) Well, that rarely happens. Entrepreneurs are people, too. They have lives, families, and financial obligations. They don't say "to hell with financial security" on a whim. They commit after careful thought, and even then they don't bet everything they have.

Harriet says she lived exclusively on pasta and salad for three years. And while she admits it is a cliché, Harriet adds that she funded her venture using her credit cards. Again, you can find examples where this is true—especially if the entrepreneur is young and has no financial commitments (no family to support, no mortgage to pay, etc.). But in the vast majority of cases, entrepreneurs don't bet everything on one roll of the dice. Like the rest of us, they simply couldn't take that big a chance.

Moving on

What are we left with, after we have addressed all these myths? Just this. Entrepreneurs, like the rest of us, want to feel that their journey is unique. And, also like the rest of us, they sometimes remember their past in more heroic (than accurate) ways. But really they are not especially different from you or us. They are not more heroic. They don't have X-ray vision that allows them to spot holes in the marketplace, and they don't have a special gene that allows them to succeed. So what makes entrepreneurs entrepreneurs? There are two overwhelming traits that jump out from the research. These can be combined and summarized in 12 words:

Entrepreneurs have a passion for discovering opportunities. Once they do, they act.

Part of that is self-evident, of course. Entrepreneurs do. They act. (If you just sit around and think of ideas for a new product or service, but don't *do* anything with those thoughts, you are not an entrepreneur. You are just someone with a lot of unrealized ideas.) The direct link between thinking and doing is the reason we have divided the book into two distinct parts: Entrepreneurial Thought *and* Entrepreneurial Action. And as we talked about earlier, that action leads to more thoughts, which, in turn, leads to more actions, which in turn leads to more thought which . . .

But none of this is extraordinary in and of itself. So are we saying that anyone can be entrepreneurial?

Absolutely.

The more we learn, the more we are convinced that *everybody can use CreAction effectively*, that entrepreneurship is not just a set of specific traits or characteristics. It is a way of looking at the world and solving problems—business problems, social problems, personal problems—just like the scientific method. As Saras points out, everybody can learn to be a scientist. Not everybody can become an Einstein, but everyone can actually learn to become more scientific in their reasoning. In the same way, we believe that everyone can become more creative or entrepreneurial in their reasoning. In fact, it is easier than becoming a scientist, because you don't need to understand differential equations. All you do, in the words of the old song (a hit for both the Beatles and Buck Owens), is "act naturally." You rediscover the way you used to think.

We'll explain why that is in the next chapter.

Takeaways from Chapter 2

1 | **Everyone is capable of employing CreAction.** While entrepreneurs are the best example of the kind of people who use CreAction effectively, you certainly don't have to be an entrepreneur to employ it.

2 | **CreAction works in non-business settings, too.** It is a logic that helps create *anything* new.

3 | **Combining CreAction and Prediction** gives you the greatest chance of success.

3 Underscoring the difference between CreAction and the kind of reasoning we are used to: Prediction

It is extremely helpful to know where each works best.

Let's take one full step back, in order to make going forward a whole lot easier.

As we have said, successful entrepreneurs employ the two kinds of reasoning we have been talking about—Prediction and CreAction.

Before we go any further, we want to stress that neither way of thinking is superior to the other. And in fact you need both if you are going to be as successful as possible. (We pointed out in the Introduction that we have a term for when you employ both successfully in parallel: Entrepreneurial Thought and Action.)

But while both approaches are valuable, most of us are less familiar with CreAction, and thus by default we lapse into overuse of Prediction. That's a key reason we want to stop here and look at **both** in detail.

Prediction reasoning

Prediction is the kind of thinking we have all been trained to do since kindergarten. **It is a pattern of thinking and acting based on the assumption that the future is going to be similar to the present and the immediate past**. It involves inferring and extrapolating from what has come before and acting based on what you think the future is going to be like.

> Why do we need to understand a new kind of reasoning? Because the future is not as predictable as we would like.

When we use Prediction in business (or business classes) or just in life in general, we begin with a goal in mind—we want to create a new and better widget, or a unique service, or a new neighborhood recreation center—with a given set of means. ("Here are the resources we have—the money, people, time, etc.—available to build that widget, create that service, or make that new building happen.")

Then with both the goal and the resources identified, we set off to identify the optimal—fastest, cheapest, most efficient, etc.—path to achieving our objective. The make-vs.-buy decision in production, or choosing the target with the highest potential return in marketing, or creating a portfolio with the lowest risk in finance, or even hiring the best person to run the local rec center, are all examples of problems that call for the use of Prediction. And, as we've said, this is the stuff we are familiar with: deductive logic; rules of thumb; mathematical models.

CreAction (Creation reasoning)

CreAction, however, does not necessarily begin with a specific goal. (You know you want to leave your job and go off on your own, but you have absolutely no idea what company you want to start.) It is driven by desire and action and is based on the means, or resources, we have at hand.

When you go about making a list of those resources, it looks like this:

- Who am I?

- What do I know?

- What resources do I have at hand?

- Who do I know that I can collaborate or share the risk with?

(We will expand on all these bullet points in the Chapter 5.)

CreAction allows you to take smart steps into an unknowable future in order to discover and/or invent that future as you go. In other words, you are going to create the world going forward (hence the name). Your goals emerge over time from your insights and aspirations, from the people that you partner with, and through what you learn by taking action.

Let's look at the way people who employ CreAction use it in practice. But before we do, let's make a point that is probably obvious. As we discuss the differences between CreAction and Prediction we will draw clear, bright lines. And that can make it sound as if you would use one form of reasoning exclusively in one situation, and the other when faced with something else. The fact is people reciprocate between the two often in solving the same problem.

For example, imagine you see an attractive someone across the room. Based on the animated way they are chatting with friends, you predict they would be an interesting person to get to know. You could stay in the Prediction mode and spend a lot of time trying to figure out the perfect opening line, or you could just take action by walking over, saying hi, and seeing what happens.

One more quick example to make the point. You're hungry and so head down to the supermarket to buy some potato chips. As you walk there, you discover they have closed the road off for a parade that you had forgotten about, and so you need to detour around the block. Halfway around you see your favorite pasta shop. Pasta, yum! And so you satisfy your hunger not by having a snack of potato chips, as you originally intended, but by having lunch (pasta primavera).

In writing a book it's hard to bounce back and forth in describing two different things—in this case Prediction and CreAction—so we are discussing them one at a time. Just remember, in solving a particular challenge in the "real world" you will be constantly alternating between the two, whether you are trying to start a new company or meet someone new.

How do you see the future?

The fundamental difference between CreAction and Prediction boils down to the way you think about the future. Prediction is, as Saras says, based on the premise that *to the extent that we can predict the future, we can control it.* That's why both academics and businesspeople spend enormous amounts of brainpower and resources developing predictive models, algorithms, and the like.

Those who employ CreAction take an entirely different mental

> People who employ CreAction believe the future can be shaped by human action. What naturally follows from that thought is this one: If we can control the future, we don't have to waste energy trying to predict it.

posture: *To the extent that we can make the future through our actions, we don't need to predict it.*

Let's summarize the fundamental difference between **Prediction** and **CreAction** in a single chart.

CONTRASTING PREDICTION AND CREACTION

View of the Future

Prediction: *Prediction.* The future is a continuation of the past and can be reasonably predicted. Goals are achieved by extrapolating from the past and positioning yourself to catch the wave. Accuracy of prediction is paramount.

CreAction: *Creation.* The future is contingent on human action. Unpredictability itself is seen as a resource. Goals are achieved by doing the doable and continually transforming current realities into new and unforeseen possibilities.

Basis for Commitment & Action

Prediction: *Goals.* Clarity of goals drives resource acquisition and management. What means do I need to assemble to achieve these goals?

CreAction: *Means at hand.* What effects can I create with the means I have?

Prediction: *Think a lot.* Act only once the logic is fully in place to achieve the end. The next step is based on the previous thought.

CreAction: *Start acting as soon as you can,* as soon as it's logical to take the next step. The next step is based on the new reality, which results from your action.

Prediction: *Should.* Do what you ought to do based on what's "best." Goals determine sub-goals and actions. Thorough analysis precedes action. Time and/or other resources are invested in upfront information-gathering. (*Optimizing*)

CreAction: *Want (and can).* Do what you want and are able to do, which is not necessarily "best." Your desires, means, and the actual commitments of others form the sub-goals. Actions and interactions with others precede and drive the process of CreAction. Creative energies focus on building a venture with virtually no resources invested. (*Satisficing*)

Attitude toward Investment & Risk

Prediction: *Expected return.* Calculate upside potential and pursue (risk-adjusted) best opportunity. Risk management involves the careful avoidance of failure.

CreAction: *Affordable loss.* Calculate downside potential and invest no more than you want or can afford to lose. Risk management involves keeping failures small and having them happen early, and then learning from them for future success. Each stakeholder invests only what he or she can afford to or is willing to lose.

Dealing with Unexpected

Prediction: *Bring plan back on track.*

CreAction: *Redesign plan* and even, sometimes, your desires in order to profit from surprises.

Attitude toward Others

Prediction: *Competition.* Constrain task relationships with customers and suppliers to what is necessary. The likelihood of delivering on your targets dictates whom to bring on board.

CreAction: *Partnership.* Build your market together with customers, suppliers, and even prospective competitors. The people who come on board help determine the goals and shape of the venture and its market.

Underlying Logic

Prediction: *To the extent we can predict the future, we can control it.*

CreAction: *To the extent we can create the future, we do not need to predict it.*

Sarasvathy, Schlesinger, Kiefer and Brown

Okay, that list can seem a bit dry (and aimed at those who are used to using Prediction). If you want another way of thinking about the differences between Prediction and CreAction, get your head out of this book and head into the kitchen and rattle those pots and pans. Let's talk about how you see the difference in your own home.

CreAction is as close as your kitchen

There are two general approaches to cooking. One is to start with a dish you want to make, find a great recipe, get the ingredients, and make it. That would be the classic Prediction approach. You have a pretty solid idea of what the end result is going to be. You want to make a seven-cheese lasagna, and you end up doing just that.

In terms of the chart we just saw: You would start with your goal in mind (creating a lasagna); you would determine what assets you would need to make that goal a reality (the seven cheeses, pasta, tomato sauce, etc.); and then you would set off to accomplish the goal (by following a well-tested recipe).

The other way is to walk into the kitchen, open the refrigerator, find stuff, and figure out what to make. As you set off to make dinner, you would be looking at the means at hand (the ingredients you have) and not a specific goal (such as making a lasagna) in trying to determine what you are going to eat.

How do you deal with an unpredictable future? The answer depends on where you believe the future comes from. Do you expect it to be a continuation of the past? If it is, Prediction helps to tell you what's ahead and will allow you to position yourself accordingly. But if you believe the future won't be like the past—or you simply have no way of knowing—you want to employ CreAction.

No matter where you are—stumbling around the kitchen, or stumbling around the marketplace—you are much more likely to come up with a new dish that you might not have actually planned to make using CreAction.

So, it's not really a question of whether this is better than that. It is just the way entrepreneurs do it. They work with what they have and they look around and say, "What can I do with this?" That is an increasingly valuable skill set to have as the world grows progressively harder to predict.

Again, let us underscore that entrepreneurs use either (or both) Prediction and/or CreAction, depending on what the circumstances call for. But they show a preference for CreAction in the early stages of a new venture. And, in fact, research shows that they prefer it 89% of the time in the course of building their companies. (By contrast, corporate managers favor Prediction as much as 81% of the time.)

This should seem familiar

You may find that CreAction comes easily to you as you start to play with the concepts in this book. That shouldn't be surprising. It's the way we thought at birth. As an infant/toddler/preschooler, everything you confronted for the first time was an unknown. Because it was, you tried certain things. You tried to walk. You put your finger in a light socket. And as a result of your actions, certain things happened. Some good. (Walking.) Some bad. (That shocking light socket.) But that is how you dealt with an unknowable universe. You took small steps.

This way of approaching life has become unfamiliar to us over time, because:

1. It has been replaced by the Prediction reasoning used to explain reading, writing, and arithmetic, and just about everything else in school.

2. Most of our daily chores and actions take place within an extremely predictable universe.

But, CreAction has remained within you. In other words, you already know how to think this way.

To prove that, think about how you would proceed if you were heading off on a journey into the unknown (which of course is another way of describing starting a company or any other new venture).

Before leaving you would:

1. Do what you could to minimize risk. (You'd make sure you were in the best of health; you would have gathered any resources you could anticipate needing; you would have done all the research you possibly could about what you were about to face.)

2. Take small steps to keep from stumbling into a mess you could not immediately get out of.

3. Pause after you took those small steps to make sure you were on solid and safe ground.

4. Build off of what you discovered after taking each of those safe, small steps.

5. Make sure you had friends to call on to help you get there (and in case you got into trouble).

In other words, you would conduct a series of fast, low-cost/low-risk experiments to find out exactly what you are facing at each step of the journey, holding back resources to make sure that any stumble or failure wouldn't be fatal.

Well, that is exactly the course of action entrepreneurs take in the real world. You can see evidence of this if we go back to our starting-a-salsa-company example. But this time, instead of using the path to market that was described in the faux magazine piece (the one that contained all the entrepreneurial myths that turned out to be exactly that—myths), let's talk about what probably would have happened in the real world based on our study of how entrepreneurs think and behave.

We will begin with the same premise: Harriet Harrison wants to find an opportunity to start a business of her own. But instead of chucking everything and starting from scratch, odds are she would have inched toward entrepreneurship by doing her research on nights and weekends and pondering things during her day job. (This is an example of doing all the preparation work and planning up front.)

Then, having had the light bulb go on ("she knew the world wanted a smoother, sweeter salsa"), she probably would **not** have locked herself in her kitchen for a year to create the perfect salsa. Rather, she probably would have come up with two or three recipes she liked and tried them out on family and friends. If they liked them, she would then start trying to sell the salsa (an example of taking a small, smart step). Whichever sold best at weekend craft fairs or church bazaars—places where she could set up shop at little or no cost on nights and weekends (so she wouldn't have to quit her day job)—would be the one she would try to sell in new markets. (If the other two also appealed to customers, they might become her second or third products.)

If none of the three showed satisfactory sales, she would have scrapped them all—she wouldn't have invested all that much, up until this point, so the loss would not have been too great—and either gone back to the drawing board or quit the venture and tried something else.

> Most business schools teach potential entrepreneurs an extremely linear, analytic process—idea, market research, business plan, financing, etc.—with the caveat, of course, that surprises will happen along the way. Seasoned entrepreneurs, however, know that surprises are not deviations from the path. They are the norm.

As for distribution, she might have friends in different parts of the country sell it for her, or done deals with distributors who would receive a percentage of each jar sold instead of a   at fee. She would then use the money she received from the initial sales to fund her business. (Not only would that be an example of having friends standing by, it also means you don't need to rack up tens of thousands of dollars in credit card debt to get a venture going.)

Again, if none of this worked, she would not be out very much money or time. Every step of the process was designed to see if she was on the right path.

This version of Harriet's journey wouldn't make for a dramatic magazine article. But it is representative of how entrepreneurs think with CreAction, and it uses a different kind of logic than we were taught in school. It is an extremely useful tool if you want to create something new . . . and that is where we turn our attention next.

YOU MUST REMEMBER THIS
Takeaways from Chapter 3

1 | **Prediction, the kind of thinking that works** extremely well when the future will be similar to the past, increasingly fails us in an environment where things become more and more uncertain.

2 | **CreAction, the kind of reasoning we did before we entered school**, is ideal when the only way to know the future is to step into it by acting. One approach is not better than the other. We need both.

3 | **The fact that entrepreneurs use CreAction as much as they do isn't surprising.** CreAction is particularly well suited when the future is unknowable, essentially impossible to predict, or when you are trying to create something utterly new. In this realm Prediction is not appropriate; it does not and cannot work, since there is no—or very little—history to draw on to try to predict what the future will be like.

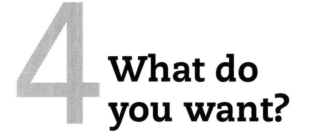

CHAPTER

What do
you want?

Without an overwhelming desire to make
something happen, the odds are nothing will.
You must truly want to bring something into being.
Without that desire nothing else matters . . . or
occurs. So, the starting point is this: What do you
truly want to create?

Okay. We've convinced you that everyone, most notably you,
has the ability to create something new. And you may even have
some sort of idea of what you'd like to create. That concept could
be as vague as "I want to do something to make people healthier,"
or as specific as selling a ketchup-like salsa.

Does all this make you an entrepreneur?

Obviously not.

Same question, different context. Maybe you don't want to do
anything involving commerce. But you have an idea for a nonprofit
that can bridge racial differences, or an outreach program for kids.

Do those ideas make you a social entrepreneur or change agent?

Again, obviously not.

In both cases you need to act. You need to do something with your idea. As we said in Chapter 1, thinking is terrific, but absolutely nothing happens unless you take smart steps to translate your ideas into action. If all you do is think about potential companies you could start, services you could provide, or how you could make the world around you a better place, you are no different than all those annoying people who come up to a novelist at a party and say, "I always wanted to write a book; I have a great idea, it's about . . ." and never put their fingers on a keyboard or pen to paper.

You need to put your thoughts into action to see if you are right about there being a potential audience/customer for your ideas (and learn what you need to change if there is not). We will talk all about how action trumps thinking a bit later in the book. But before we do, we need to know what causes people to act. We need to know why some people feel compelled to move from thinking to doing, a step that the rest of the world—those folks who *think* they have a good idea for a book, nonprofit, website, retail concept, or civic initiative—never makes.

Going right to the source

If you ask entrepreneurs of any stripe what made them get started, you will get different answers: "I always knew I wanted to do this;" "I sort of stumbled into it;" "I wanted to make a lot of money, and this idea was the way to do it." "I never really cared about making a lot of money. This was a way to help people."

But if you search for commonality, it is easy to find. They **wanted** to do it; often they say they **had** to do it; they felt compelled. To reduce it to a word, what caused them to act was **desire**. They had a desire—sometimes an overwhelming desire, but always, at the very least, a desire—to act, to create something.

Desire is a word we rarely use in connection with commerce. And when it surfaces, people are quick to try to eliminate it because it sounds squishy, unbusiness-like, and, of course, hard to quantify and teach. But it is the right word, defined as "a longing or craving, as for something that brings satisfaction or enjoyment." Its synonyms are even more accurately descriptive: *aspiration, longing, passion,* and *yearning,* language that—as the *Random House Dictionary of the English Language (unabridged, second edition)* correctly points out—"suggests feelings that impel one to the attainment or possession of something . . . that is (in reality or imagination) within reach." Desire is what compels people to create something new, something that they want to bring into being.

But what gets them to pull the trigger? All those people who come up to novelists (or artists or singers or actors or musicians) at parties presumably really do want to write a book (or paint a picture or perform). And all those people who know they have an idea for the proverbial better mousetrap say they want to make it a reality. So, why don't they? When does the desire become so strong that you have to act on it?

The answer boils down to this: You are moved to create when you have a desire to do so **and** you can see a next step that you can afford to take.

To go a bit further, the answer divides into two sides of the same coin. On the positive side, people end up creating when it is more appealing than their current situation, and/or there simply isn't much, if anything, to lose by trying something new. In other words, they see the chance to engage in something that could be potentially pleasurable at an acceptable cost.

Of course people can also be motivated to move away from something, which is the negative side of the coin. Here the motivation goes: No matter how scary or unsettling starting a new venture may be, the alternative of doing nothing is worse. My current situation makes it imperative for me do something else. (To do a bit of foreshadowing: As we will discuss in detail in a moment, this will probably not work as a motivating force long-term, but it may be sufficient to get you started.)

> Desire is the most critical resource you
> have in starting a new venture.

With the framework established, let's look at both potential "desire triggers" in detail, because as we said, if the desire isn't there, odds are nothing new is going to be created.

Let's start with the "positive."

PASSION, DESIRE, AND LOVE

We didn't list passion in the myth section of Chapter 2 (when we were talking about what everyone "knows" about entrepreneurs that turns out to be wrong), but we could have.

Entrepreneurs and people who write about them are always telling you that you need to be *passionate* about your ventures. There are at least three reasons why you should be careful with this thought.

The first has to do with what we mean by the word "passion." It is used in ways that have different meanings and can confuse the conversation. At one end of the spectrum, the word might be described as "emotionally stirring." This is a good thing. Having strong emotions about your venture is important for obvious reasons: If you don't care about what you are doing, you probably won't do it well.

At the other end of the spectrum, however, is the use of "passion" as a description of intense and often wild emotions. People get carried away with passion. People kill each other out of passion. People are blinded by passion. This kind of passion is not creative; it is destructive and detrimental.

So, while we are in favor of passion used the first (emotionally stirring) way, there is another word that, although unfamiliar in the business context, is better: love. Love, as we define it, is the yearning for the realization of the venture *on its own terms*. Caring enough about the success of the venture that you will do what it takes for it to become real. No one ever intentionally damaged something out of love.

And that brings us to the second reason love can be the right word. An essential characteristic of an entrepreneur is perseverance: the ability to picture what you are trying to create, dropping anything that distracts from or interferes with that focus. Holding something in your imagination is extremely challenging when you're relying upon your intellect, telling yourself it is a "good idea" or that you "should" keep at it. But it is unavoidable if it's something that you actually care about.

Think about the last time you were in love. It was impossible not to think about the loved one. Think about your children. It's impossible to not repeatedly over the course of the day call their well-being into your mind. Love of the venture has the same power. Focusing attention on what you want to create and dropping anything that distracts you is the most natural thing in the world when you are emotionally stirred by love, or passion, or whatever term you might prefer.

Finally, even if passion were required, it is of no practical use to know that. You cannot synthesize or fake desire. When was the last time you tried to want something you didn't want or love someone that you didn't love?

You can't manipulate yourself into caring. We are either (in the rare case) instantaneously smitten (for some, the birth of a child), or, more often, we come to care about things or people over time (our best friends). Desire is not something that we self-consciously create; it is something that we are gifted with. Telling someone that they have to be passionate about some-thing is worthless advice because no one can do anything with it. Even worse, it is potentially harmful, because you could be left with the impression that you better not start that new ven-ture unless you are passionate about it. Far better to get started with whatever desire you have, and over time you may be graced with love.

"What if"

When inspiration strikes it is always unique, but the spark that gets people to act is always familiar. They suddenly say to themselves:

"I wonder what would happen if . . ." or

"It might be fun to . . ." or

"Wouldn't it be neat if . . ." or

"This idea has me by the throat and I need to do something with it to see how it plays out."

Whether the idea is all encompassing ("it has me by the throat") or appears as an entertaining notion ("wouldn't it be fun if . . ."), the person is compelled (or intrigued enough) to take action. We aren't talking about selling everything they own and going into the new venture whole hog. They have no intention of quitting their day job and spending every waking moment on making this new thing a reality. (See our discussion of "entrepreneurial myths" in Chapter 2.) Rather, they are thinking, "Let me take a first step, just enough to cause action, toward making this idea a reality. And if I like the results, I'll take another."

Put differently, they don't see a lot of downside in getting underway. (See Chapter 7 on affordable loss.) Think about all the people who created dot-coms during the late 1990s and into the early 2000s. Invariably, when asked whether they found the idea of starting their own company risky, they said something like "if it doesn't work out, I can always go back to what I was doing." The cynics will point out that a lot of those people did end up going back to their former sources of employment once the tech bubble burst. To which we say: true, but an awful lot of companies that got started back then are still up and running. As the Kauffman Foundation, which is devoted to promoting entrepreneurship and innovation, points out, between 1980 and 2005 virtually all new jobs in the U.S.—about 40 million in total—were created by firms that were five years old or less. Netting out layoffs, retirements, and the number of people who moved from one big company to another, **established firms did not create a single job**.

"I can't stand it"

The negative impetus is also easy to understand. People sometimes start a business because their current situation feels, or truly is, awful, and they can't stand the status quo. They are working at a job they despise; they desperately need more money; they simply hate the answer they give when someone asks "what do you do to make a living?" You get the idea. Anything, even plunging into the unknown, is better than what they are doing now.

Now, getting rid of something you don't want can be a great spur to action. It can get you going in another direction. But the problem is that it is not great as a force to sustain you over time.

It is always more desirable to move toward something you truly want than to move away from something you hate.

When you're doing something that you want, the quality of energy you bring to the activity is entirely different than when you are doing something you feel obligated to do, or something that is simply a (slightly) better alternative than the awful status quo you face.

At some point, if eeing a negative situation is why you have chosen to create something new, the switch will have to ip. You will have to truly want to continue working on the idea, otherwise you probably will lose the desire to see it through. Ironically, if that happens, you could end up in exactly the same place you started, hating how you are spending your days. There are exceptions. There are people who succeed "to show everyone who said I couldn't they were wrong." However, those people tend to be a) exceptional indeed and b) not very happy, despite their success.

But the point at which you have to ip the switch is down the line. As we said, even desperation could be enough to get you started.

Why is this important?

There are four questions you might ask before starting any new venture:

1. Is it doable? (Is it feasible and within the realm of reality?) (Notice this is a prediction, which underscores the fact that CreAction and Prediction can work together.)

2. Do I believe I can do it? (This is Prediction, too.)

3. Is it worth doing? (Will there be a market for what I want to sell? Is there potential to turn a profit? Will people appreciate what I am trying to do? In other words, does it make sense to put in all this effort?)

4. Do I want to do it?

But the last is the only one that really matters: **Do I want to do it?**

Why? Because if you think it through, you'll realize that in a world where you can't predict the future, the answers to the first three questions are all the same: "There is no way of telling."

In the unpredictable world, you won't know if you can do it until you actually try—so that takes care of the first two queries—and you can do all the market research you want, or ask EVERYONE what they think about your idea, but the only way to truly discover if someone is going to react positively to what you want to do is to take an action and see what happens. There is just no way to predict with any level of certainty the answers to questions one, two, and three. Until you act, you won't know.

However, none of that matters until—and unless—you answer the fourth question: Do you want to do it? If you don't, there is simply no way you are going to give the new venture a good effort. Creating something new is hard enough when you give it everything you have; it is near impossible when your heart isn't in it.

Role of desire in assessing risk

Conversely, if you really want to do something, everything gets reframed. The negative emotional response to all the unknowns is reduced. The reality hasn't changed. You still don't know what is out there, but you'll find a way around the problem, because you want to. (See Chapter 9.)

Let us give you two almost identical situations to show how this plays out. In situation #1, you work for an agricultural firm, and your boss gives you the assignment of figuring out how to sell the company's farm equipment to Cuba—and you haven't a clue if it can be done.

Here's how our four questions play out:

Is it doable? There is a trade embargo.

Can you do it? You haven't a clue how to set up a distribution network in a communist country.

Is it worth doing? Who knows the size of the market?

Do you want to do it? Well, no. It's the boss's idea.

Situation #2 is exactly the same. The only difference is it is your idea. **You** are the one who wants to sell agricultural equipment to Cuba. You think there is a huge opportunity and you have a compelling desire to give it a try.

What's the likely result in both cases? It isn't a hard question.

In the first situation, where desire is not part of the equation, you aren't in any hurry to do anything because the situation is so uncertain and unknown. You will keep thinking about what you are up against and search for more data. You will put it at the very bottom of your "to do" pile and if your boss never follows up, you may never take any real action.

But the presence of desire alters all of that. Because **you want** to do it, you are much more likely to take a small, first smart step toward solving the challenge. For example, you establish an office in Canada, (Please note: Your authors are not advocating circumventing U.S. trade embargoes.), which does allow trade with Cuba, and start setting up meetings with the Minister of Agriculture's staff. And as we see later (in Chapter 8), your passion for creating something new will make it far easier to get others to come along with you as either investors or employees. Nobody will be committed to what you're doing if they don't see your desire, your belief in your idea, and your willingness to try to accomplish it.

We've made the case that desire is critical. And odds are you will be filled with desire as you get underway in whatever new venture you start. But what happens if that desire fades over time? It would be nice to think that you will be as enthusiastic about your new venture on days 91 and 361 as you were on day 1. But what happens if you are not? Is that a bad thing?

Not necessarily.

The day-to-day reality of building a business or creating anything new can be wearing, so a temporary loss of enthusiasm is natural. And even if you decide to step away from the project for a few days, or even a few months, that isn't a sign of trouble in and of itself. Taking a break is healthy and it might help you gain perspective.

However, if the loss of desire seems permanent, it is time to do something else. Again, this is common too. We see it all the time with entrepreneurs who are full of desire when they are in the process of getting their companies up and running and then lose zeal when the firm is fully underway. When that happens, it is time for them to leave—either sell or turn the running of the company over to a professional manager—and do something else.

A bit of foreshadowing

We will talk in the next section about how CreAction has a logic composed of four elements: getting started quickly with the means at hand; assessing how much you can afford to lose; drawing in committed stakeholders; and turning obstacles into assets and opportunities. And we will point out there is a bias toward action (so that the entrepreneur can learn from those actions and then act again based on what they learned in a continuing acting/learning loop).

But none of that is going to happen, unless there is a desire.

Everything we will talk about from here on out is driven by desire. The presence of desire powerfully amplifies the impact of each of the four steps.

Without it, nothing happens.

YOU MUST REMEMBER THIS
Takeaways from Chapter 4

1 | **Nothing happens until you take that first smart step.** All the ideas in the world don't mean a thing unless you do something with them. If you don't act, all you have is a bunch of ideas.

2 | **But before you act . . .** you need to know what you want. If you don't have a strong desire, odds are you will never see your idea through.

3 | **You don't need to be obsessed or even in love with the idea**, but there must be some reason pushing you forward. Otherwise, nothing will happen.

II Entrepreneurial Action

5 Act quickly with the means at hand

The first of the four fundamental building blocks of CreAction.

Once you truly have the desire to create something new, where do you start?

Well, the very fact that you are asking the question shows you are on the right track. The people who excel at CreAction don't spend months or years assembling resources. They begin with the means at hand.

What does that inventory include? The short answer: anything that might be relevant. We know, that's vague. The answer to the following three questions can help identify the specifics:

- **Who am I?** What traits, tastes, and inclinations do I have that I can draw on in starting a new venture?

- **What do I know?** This includes your education, training, experience, and expertise.

- **Who do I know?** What people can I draw upon—in my personal, social, and professional networks—to help this new idea succeed?

These may not be the very first things people starting a new venture ask. They could say, "Where am I going to get the money to fund this thing?" (if funding is required); or "Is now the time to re-locate, before I set up shop?" You can start your journey anywhere. But no matter where they start, the people who are best at creating new ventures know the answers to these questions very early in the process.

That should not be surprising. As we discussed, CreAction, the kind of reasoning most favored by entrepreneurs and others plunging into the unknown, is based on the means they have at hand. And by asking, "Who am I?"; "What do I know?"; and "Who do I know?", they are taking stock of some of the key means at their disposal.

Because these three questions are so important, let's look at each in more detail.

Who am I?

While you can start anywhere in determining what means are available to you, this is a logical place to begin. In asking "who am I," you are really trying to find out: what kind of a person am I; what kinds of things turn me on; what really matters to me; and what kind of things will I not do because they either go against my values, or I just don't find them interesting enough to invest any time in.

Answering these questions gives you a sense of self, which helps you to quickly eliminate ideas that don't "fit." ("Hmm. This idea of finding smart minority kids and steering them to the best possible colleges is interesting, but I really need to make a lot of money. So as intriguing as the concept is, it won't provide me with a big income. I need to find something else.") You end up knowing what you want to do—and what you don't.

That is hugely important, of course. What enables you to create is the ability to focus your attention. If you are distracted, disinterested, or dealing with something that doesn't excite you, it is hard to focus. Creating something worthwhile under those conditions is extremely difficult.

> We often are unaware of all our strengths . . . and weaknesses. Ask others to talk to you about what you are good at (and what you are not). You don't need to accept what they say as gospel; but it may be easier for them to see things about you than you can.

Conversely, when you are in love with an idea, your attention takes care of itself. (This ties back to our earlier discussion about desire.) But the big point here is self-awareness is key. You need to know what you want, and what you don't.

What do I know?

You never know where the insight that leads to an opportunity will come from. That is why mentally cataloging what you know is so important. For example, you may have gone to a school known for its rigor in math and the hard sciences. But it turns out that even though your degree is in engineering, you gain the most joy in your life by bringing together like-minded people. That's why in thinking about what you know, you want to think about your personal as well as your professional life.

Why make such an extensive list? When you operate in the area of unknowability—and remember, at this point in the process you have no clear idea of exactly what venture you will be starting, or even if you are actually going to end up starting one— you don't know what is relevant. It is not always clear beforehand which pieces of information are worth paying attention to and which are not. Everything is potentially important, at least initially. It is only later (or after the fact) that the things that are superuous become clear.

TO HELP YOUR THINKING

One of the best opening lines of any book is the first sentence of *Baby and Child Care* by Dr. Benjamin Spock. He wrote: "You know more than you think you do."

That is true about parents. And it's certainly true about anyone thinking about starting something new. As a way to help think about what you truly know, break down the task by categories.

Ask, what do I know:
- Professionally?
- From my training?
- Personally?
- About the world around me?

From there, you can ask:
- What aptitudes do I have; what am I good at?
- What did I learn in school that can help me?
- What have I learned from my personal and professional experiences?

We guarantee your answers to each question will trigger more than three potential ideas to pursue. (If they don't, keep asking.)

Who do I know?

Serial entrepreneurs—people who have started multiple business-es successfully—involve others in their new projects from the con-ception of the idea. They are looking to leverage their resources (there is no reason to reinvent the wheel when a friend of a friend owns the world's biggest wheel store), and it is an excellent way to spread risk. (We will talk about this in Chapter 8.)

What works for them should work for you, whether you are starting a business or trying to change an organization or starting a new club at your school. That's why determining who you know is so important.

TO HELP YOUR THINKING (II)

If you have ever planned a wedding, or had to organize a huge party for all your friends and acquaintances, you are well aware that you know a lot more people than you think you do.

To help you generate a definitive list, you may want to start thinking of people you know by category.

Ask, who do I know:
- Personally?
- Socially?
- Professionally?

From there, you can add names by category, such as:
- People with money (if you need money for what you plan to do)
- People who want to take risks
- People who know other people
- People who would be fun to work with
- People who can get stuff done

And then you can sort by specific skills, by asking (if you are starting a company) who do I know who knows a lot about:
- Finance?
- Marketing?
- Recruiting?
- Building a company?

Or if you are starting a new course at the local community college, who can:
- Get the word out?
- Help me double check that I have covered everything I want to teach?
- Handle the paperwork?

There is another important point to make about this. Bringing in other people early inevitably changes the final result. What you end up deciding to create will be the combined result of not only your imagination and aspirations, but also those of all the people you will have interacted with over the course of the process. CreAction lives and breathes execution. Plans are made and unmade and revised and recast through action and interaction with others on a daily basis.

Current reality

Everything you have done up until this point has been done in the context of current reality, i.e., you have taken stock of the world around you as it really is. That's terrific, and you should keep that current reality front and center in your mind as you continue to act.

When you are heading off into the unknown, understanding current reality is a very, very, very good idea.

This is important because if you don't, you are bound to either be disappointed or give up too soon. Let us give you examples of each. Sometimes people who are trying to create something assume it will be relatively easy to get the government to come along as a partner. "It will only cost each taxpayer $1.34," they say about a well-intentioned program, or they might contend that a new kind of wellness program "will pay for itself" (in reduced long-term health care costs).

Both statements could be absolutely true, but when it comes to government spending, that is irrelevant. You need to know what politicians will and will not fund.

If, on the other hand, you just assume the world is stuck in its ways, you could shortchange a potential opportunity. Coffee sales had been steadily declining for years before Howard Schultz created Starbucks. People assumed individuals wouldn't pay for television or radio before cable and Sirius/XM came along. The United States Postal Service saw no reason to create overnight mail, which allowed Fred Smith to start FedEx.

Takeaways from Chapter 5

1 | **Once you know what you want**, you of course need to figure out how to get it. That means very early on you need to know what resources you have. You can find out by asking the questions: who am I; what do I know; and who do I know.

2 | **A key part of moving forward is understanding current reality.** The way the world really is not the way you would like it to be. You might, indeed, be able to change the world. But to do that, you need to understand where the world is now. This can be an Achilles' heel for entrepreneurs. They can get so caught up in what they are trying to do that they fail to perceive current reality as clearly as they might.

3 | **Once you understand where you are and what resources are at your command, it is time to take action.**

6 Action trumps thinking

(when the future is unpredictable). That concept is the cornerstone of CreAction. Here are 16 reasons why that is true.

Notice what we stuck in parentheses in the chapter title. Action, a key part of CreAction, does indeed trump thinking *when the future can't be known with much certainty*. That simple statement makes sense, of course. If you are heading into an unknown frontier—and starting a new journey of any sort certainly qualifies in many cases—the only way to know what is out there (are there potential customers; is the market big enough; will the community like the civic venture I helped create?) is to go and find out. Thinking and creating endless "what if" scenarios doesn't help you. You can "what if" yourself to death. The only way to know for sure is to act, re ect on what you have learned, and (to gain more learning) act some more.

But before you do, double check to see that the future is as uncertain as you think; that there is, indeed, no way to predict what will happen. If there is a more than reasonable chance that the future is knowable (we will give two examples in a second so you can see exactly what we are talking about), you are better off letting Prediction dominate—and that is a good thing.

If the future is unknowable—or it will cost less to proceed than to do additional thinking—act.

Remember what we have said from the beginning. Prediction and CreAction frequently work in tandem and are equally valid on their own. By definition, that means there are certain situations where Prediction works better. You could take an egg out of the refrigerator, hold it out at arm's length, and, to find out what will happen if you drop it, take action by letting go. But there is little reason for doing so (other than to entertain a three-year-old). The laws of gravity are well known. The fact that the egg will break could have been predicted with near certainty.

Similarly, you could go out and start a transportation company tomorrow and learn by doing how many cars, trucks, motorcycles, and bicycles will be bought in a given year, and then sort those numbers by categories—coupes, convertibles, SUVs, etc.— and chart sales during economic good times and bad. But there is no reason to go through all that effort. Those numbers are readily available and future transportation sales can be estimated with reasonable certainty.

Our point is simple: When the results of thinking would lead to actions that are predictable—"I wonder how many high-end sports cars I could sell in a year during an economic slump"—let predictive thinking dominate (supplementing it with CreAction as necessary). You can expect Prediction to give you a solid result, i.e., you know the uncooked egg will crack when it hits the oor, and you can come up with numbers that will project fairly accurately how many of a specific type of car you are likely to sell in a given period.

But in the face of unknowability—what is the market for motorized skateboards with training wheels, or a four-wheel type of

Segway; things that don't yet exist—you need to do a lot of learning before you can know whether there is a market. And often the fastest/easiest/most effective way to get that learning is by acting.

Action leads to evidence, which becomes fodder for new thinking. Which leads to (more) evidence, which becomes (additional) fodder for even more thinking. Which leads to even more action which . . .

Why?

Well here are 16 reasons:

1. **If you act, you will find out what works . . .**

2. **. . . and what doesn't.**

3. **If you never act, you will never know if you are right or wrong.** You may *think* you know, but you won't be able to point to anything concrete to prove you are right. The problem with that, as Mark Twain famously pointed out, is clear: "It ain't so much the things we don't know that get us into trouble. It's the things we know that just ain't so."

4. **If you act, you will find out if you like it** . . . with "it" being whatever the new action is . . .

5. **. . . or you don't.**

6. **Acting leads to a market reaction, which could take you in another direction.** You thought you were going to open the world's best Italian restaurant. Taking a small step toward that goal, you began hosting large dinner parties and cooking for the monthly meeting of the Elks club to try out your recipes and discover firsthand what the food service business is like. It turns out, people raved about your food, but they were surprised you didn't want to talk to them. You, in turn, were left cold by the experience. You hated interacting with people; the idea of doing all the logistics necessary (finding a place,

dealing with the constant turnover of a waitstaff, etc.) made you break out in a cold sweat, and you really didn't want to prepare more than three kinds of entrees at a time. It turns out you learned you liked the cooking part of running a restaurant but weren't crazy about all the rest. Your action—the decision to take steps toward starting a restaurant—caused a market reaction—they loved the food but found you to be a cold fish; you loved the cooking but could do without everything else—has convinced you to go into high-end catering and hire someone to deal with the clients.

7. **As you act, you can find people to come along with you.** For example, in talking to your suppliers, you ended up meeting the world's most organized person. She now runs the day-to-day operations of your catering business and is a 10% owner.

8. **As you act, you can find ways to do things faster, cheaper, better.** You discover, after making your world-famous chicken Parmesan 50 times, that you can prepare the dish in eight steps instead of eleven.

9. **If you act, you won't spend the rest of your life going, "I wonder what would have happened if . . ."**

10. **If all you do is think, you are less interesting as a person.** Who would you rather sit next to on a plane, someone who started a successful rock-climbing store (or even an unsuccessful one), or someone who only thought about it?

11. **If all you ever do is think about stuff**, you can gain tons of theoretical knowledge, but none from the real world. You become like that woman in the fable who knows the price of everything but the value of nothing. In other words, if all you ever do is think . . .

12. **. . . all you do is think.**

13. **Action always leads to evidence.** You act, therefore something changes, and in observing that reaction you gain

knowledge. (Hmm, if I drop an egg from shoulder height, it shatters.) Thinking doesn't lead to proof—or messy oors. As Scott Cook, the founder of Intuit, says: "Evidence is better than anyone's intuition."

14. **If you act, you know what is real.** You always want to know what's real.

15. **Talking to people is acting** . . . at zero cost. You can learn an awful lot, and it usually doesn't cost you a thing. (Just make sure you act on what you learn.)

16. **It *seems* the cost of doing more thought, before you pull the trigger, is zero.** And from a dollars-and-cents point of view that may be right. But there is a huge opportunity cost. While you are still thinking, somebody else could be stealing your market or the opportunity itself may end.

There are some rules of thumb about a CreAction step. You want your next step to have no obvious aw, and you should believe that it will at least get you closer to what you want. You want the steps after the next step to logically lead you to get what you want in your best estimation, and/or you want the next step to further your learning about the unknown.

Action does indeed trump thinking when you are facing an uncertain future.

For all these reasons and dozens more that you can come up with on your own, action trumps thinking when the future is highly uncertain.

Takeaways from Chapter 6

1 | **If there is no way of knowing what the future will be like, act.** It is the quickest way to learn.

2 | **When you catch yourself thinking about an issue for a very long time**, take one more second and say, "Is it time to pull the trigger?"

3 | **Take one small step toward your goal** when it is far away or difficult to accomplish. Then evaluate where you are. The Taoist touchstone is right: A journey of a thousand miles really does begin with a single step.

7 Pay only what you can afford (and want) to pay (aka affordable loss)

There is no tooth fairy, Easter bunny, or way you can start a new venture without risk. Given that, you need to decide how much you can afford to lose before you get under way. (And if you are going to fail, fail fast—and cheaply.)

Okay, we now know that when the future is unknowable to any significant degree, action trumps thinking. But what sort of action? Rushing around willy-nilly doesn't make much sense. You want to move smartly into the unknown. So, what are the smart steps to take?

Here, again, we can learn from serial entrepreneurs. They have developed terrific ways to limit potential losses as they start new ventures. That fact surprises many people because, as we talked about in Chapter 2, if all you did was read the popular press you'd think that successful entrepreneurs love risk. Faced with the edge of a cliff, they would prefer jumping off with a homemade parachute made of bedsheets to standing still.

That's simply not true. They like ropes and harnesses! More

specifically, serial entrepreneurs prefer measured steps. They don't like risk. They accept it as part of the game and are adept at reducing it.

People who have started one or more ventures will tell you: You need to know how much you can afford to lose before you even start thinking about starting something new. And you need to do everything possible to make sure you don't exceed that figure.

They do that by adhering to the basic principles of risk management: If you're going to play in a game with uncertain outcomes, 1) don't pay/bet more than what you can expect as a return, and 2) don't pay/bet more than you can afford to lose.

Both of those ideas can be summed up with the phrase "affordable loss," a concept where you calculate the potential downside of whatever risk you are about to take—such as starting a new company or some other venture that is going to consume a lot of your time, capital, or other assets—and put on the line no more than you can afford and are willing to lose.

How pivotal is the idea of affordable loss? Consider this from Sarasvathy's study of serial entrepreneurs. Of all the people she studied, not one before they started "tried to garner specific information about potential returns or predict an ideal level of investment for their projects. Instead they wanted to spend only what they could afford to lose."

The concept of affordable loss dovetails with two concepts we have already discussed. In asking "what can I afford to lose," you are taking stock of your current reality. And by determining what you are willing (and prepared) to lose, you are double-checking your level of desire.

The serial entrepreneur's approach to affordable loss is good advice for the rest of us. Your objective should be to try to obtain your goal as cheaply and quickly as possible, with the lowest risk. You want to remain in the game as long as you can, which means you will want to draw on other people's money and resources.

So, as you prepare to take action, you need to ask two questions to make sure you stay within the bounds of your affordable loss.

1. What can I **afford** to pay to take the next step (which is based on *current reality*), and

2. What am I **willing** to pay to take the next step (which is, of course, based on *desire*)?

Now the costs we are talking about go beyond the financial. In fact, there are five:

1. **Money.** This is the most obvious, of course. Getting a new venture up and running can be costly . . . and you don't want it to be, if there is any way to help it.

2. **Time.** The people who start successful companies guard their time as much as they do their money. And just like they put a dollar figure on the amount of money they are prepared to lose, they put a limit on the time they are willing to invest. "I am willing to give this idea six months to see if it will work."

3. a) **Reputation (in the market).** We all have a professional reputation, although when you are first starting out, it may be extremely slight. There is nothing wrong with failing if the idea you tried was worthy and you were sufficiently committed to it. But if you are seen as someone who doesn't think things through, or who can't raise and/or conserve resources, that failure can seriously hurt you in whatever you do next. You may find it far harder to raise money or even to get another opportunity. Damaging your professional reputation can be a huge cost.

b) **Reputation (personal).** People may hate the question "what do you do for a living," arguing (correctly) that they are more than their job. Still, how people see you is, in part, shaped by how you earn your income. You don't want your new venture to be an embarrassment, which could affect your self-esteem, or fail to represent who you truly are.

4. **Missed opportunities.** If you are working to start X, you cannot be working on Y at exactly the same moment, and Y, potentially, could be a far better idea. In business, this is known as an "opportunity cost." Entrepreneurs recognize two other opportunity costs: the price to be paid for delay—someone else might conceive and implement your idea. And the price to be paid for inaction—you might spend the rest of your life in a job you hate, or miss a great opportunity to make a once-in-a-lifetime contribution.

5. **Family, friends, and your communities.** This is similar to the personal reputation discussion above, but closer to home. Much closer. Of course, you don't want to hurt your standing with those near and dear to you, or within your church, or civic group, or. . . . Unintelligent or frequent failures are embarrassing and carry psychosocial consequences. Moreover, one of the primary sources of funding for a new venture comes from your family and friends, and you certainly don't want to waste their money, especially if it comes from your in-laws. And all the time you will be spending on the new venture will keep you away from kith and kin, so you want to choose whatever you plan to do extremely carefully to make that loss of spending time with them worthwhile.

MONEY, MONEY, MONEY

The people who start successful companies time after time really do go into a venture thinking, "I can afford to lose X dollars on this and no more." But the thinking behind what X is is extremely nuanced.

For one thing, as we said, just because you can afford to lose $10,000 doesn't mean you want to. Obviously, you would prefer to lose far less—and presumably nothing—before getting under way.

For another, as we have talked about throughout, action changes everything. You may go into the venture believing you want to risk no more than $10,000, but as you get under way, you might discover that just another $2,500 could put you over the top. All of a sudden, $12,500 becomes your affordable loss figure.

Similarly, you could have said you would spend no more than three months determining if a new venture would work, but that might also change once you start.

The clear takeaway: By planning for the worst, you effectively reduce the risk inherent in a new venture down to what you find personally acceptable.

The research shows entrepreneurs are unwilling to wager on expectations of high returns or on their own ability to predict and sidestep potential problems. This means they play the game very conservatively. What's good for them is good for us.

Using CreAction may or may not reduce the chances that a new venture will fail, but there is absolutely no doubt that it will reduce the cost of failure (should there be one). If you fail, you fail cheaply. (More on this later in the chapter.)

It is worth staying with this point for one more minute, since it runs contrary to the image of entrepreneurs as people who constantly "swing for the fences," betting everything they own on new ventures. As we have seen, while that is sometimes true, most of the time it's not. In general, they either prefer the cheapest alternative or come up with creative ways of doing things at little cost to themselves. Furthermore, they explicitly see themselves as financially conservative. To quote just one example (and the emphasis in the quote is ours), "When I start something," a serial entrepreneur said, "I am always aware of what I am spending. I always go the cheap route. I cover my costs so I don't have to take any huge risks *if I can help it*."

It's extremely personal

Affordable loss does not depend on the venture, but the individual.

It varies from person to person, and may even vary during the course of someone's lifetime. (For example, you may be willing to risk more when you are young, knowing you will have decades to recover should things go wrong; less when your kids are approaching college age and you need to save every dollar you can for those upcoming tuition bills; and then more later on once those bills are behind you.)

So, notice what is going on. By allowing estimates of affordable loss to drive her decision about which venture to start, the potential entrepreneur is reducing her dependence on Prediction.

Here's why. Business has all kinds of financial measures that help determine whether a potential new project is worth funding. An important one is "expected return," which can be defined this way: "How much money will we get back on each dollar that we invest?" To calculate expected returns—a key determinate if someone using Prediction is deciding whether they want to start a venture—we have to estimate future sales and potential market risks, and then raise enough money to not only get under way but to hurdle all those obstacles your research uncovered.

In contrast, to calculate affordable loss, all we need to know is our current financial situation—how much money and other assets we have in total—and what is the absolute most we are willing to risk (read: lose). We either commit to starting the venture with that amount of money, figure out a way to do it cheaper, or figure out a way to attract additional investors (something we will talk about in Chapter 8).

Let's see how this plays out in practice. Consider the case of a man in his mid-40s who is thinking about quitting his high-paying job to start his own company. If our mythical potential entrepreneur were to follow Prediction, he would do in-depth research to estimate not only the size of the market, but all the risks and challenges he might face (competitors, changing market conditions, etc.). The more potential risks/challenges he believed he was up against, the more money he would raise to help offset them.

THE WORST THAT COULD HAPPEN

Post-mortems, or trying to determine why an idea failed, are common in business. But wouldn't "pre-mortems"—figuring out what could go wrong ahead of time—make more sense in business and any other places you are thinking of creating something new?

We think so. And we also believe it is a good example of how Prediction and CreAction work together.

Here's how a pre-mortem could work. Before you start, assume the new venture you are about to undertake has failed spectacularly. Then write down every plausible reason you can think of to explain the failure.

All this thinking—clearly an example of Prediction—will help you make a smart step as you start your venture. While it can't uncover all the potential obstacles you will face, it can unearth a number of them.

It is a very useful exercise.

Given all this, our potential entrepreneur might say, "I need $1 million to start this venture, and I hope to break even in two years. I can put in $100,000, which is all the money I have saved. So, I need to raise another $900,000 before I can start. That's assuming I can live without a salary for two years, and that I'm okay giving up all the money I would have made at my day job. Let me think about it. Hmmmm. Okay, I'm in. Let me start raising that $900,000."

In contrast, someone using CreAction would start with examining who they are, the means at hand, and what they can afford to lose. That leads to a very different interior monologue.

"I am 46. I've always wanted to be my own boss. By drawing on my own resources, and borrowing from family and friends, I have $100,000 I can commit to finally going off on my own. In the worst case, I start the company and lose every dime. If that happens, I'm out the $100,000 and go back to my old job, or get a different job within the industry and figure out a way to pay back everyone I borrowed from. I am willing to risk that. If I end up losing the money, so be it. It won't be the end of the world.

"But, if I don't take this risk now, when am I going to do it? I don't want to wake up 20 years from now and be one of those people who talk about 'what might have been.' There are few things sadder than having regrets about something you wanted to do but never did. My family is on board with me taking the risk, and while I know every new venture is a crapshoot, I feel pretty good about this. I am going to do it."

TO HELP YOUR THINKING

When it comes to determining how much you can personally risk in starting a new venture, i.e., your own affordable loss, ask yourself these questions:

- What are my assets? What do I have?
- What can I afford to lose?
- What am I willing to risk (lose)?

Note, the person who is using CreAction is not thinking "where will I get the biggest bang for the buck," or "what will lead to the most profit?" Instead, they are acting out of desire. This is something that they truly want to do. They expect to be successful. But they have set a limit on how much they are willing to risk.

> The notion of investing substantial amounts of energy in calculating expected returns in a highly uncertain world is silly. If something is unknowable, then all you are doing is making projections . . . on assumptions . . .that are contingent on guesses. You end up making seemingly rational decisions based on irrational analysis.

In this situation, what business you decide to start is based on where you are in your life and what you want. While you will certainly take into consideration things outside of your control—the "hot" field to go into, market risk, potential competition, etc.—those things will not drive your decision. What you want, and what you are willing to pay for it, will.

By allowing estimates of affordable loss to constrain your decisions about which venture to start, you are eliminating, to a large degree, your dependence on Prediction and its quest for certainty—financial and otherwise. Instead, your focus is on creating options that generate more options for the future. (This will only work, of course, if you are willing to adjust the shape of your venture. In other words, you need to adapt to your means, rather than remaining fixated on one specific goal.)

What this means

While managers are taught to analyze the market and choose target segments with the highest potential return, people starting a business using CreAction tend to find ways to reach the market with minimum expenditure of resources such as time, effort, and money. In the extreme case, that means starting a company with virtually no resources. That isn't hyperbole. Just think about all the technology companies—Hewlett-Packard and Apple among them—that began in someone's garage.

And not only do they often start on the proverbial shoestring, it is common for serial entrepreneurs not to do any traditional research before getting underway. Instead they often take a prototype to the nearest potential customer and describe in elaborate detail the ultimate features and benefits in an attempt to take an order.

Why? You learn a lot by a potential customers' reactions, the entrepreneurs believe. You find out where the obstacles are, what questions customers and potential customers have, and what you could charge. You might even get some cash! So the market research is actual selling.

Winning by losing

In addition to being willing to enter new and different markets, the concept of affordable loss provides more opportunities to start new businesses. You get more times at bat. This is true for two reasons. First, there are lower costs for getting under way. As opposed to Prediction, where you line up all your resources ahead of time, people who employ CreAction take small steps toward their goal. That both allows you to stay in the game longer and gives you the ability to rapidly adjust as you proceed. At any point in the journey, if you decide it isn't going to work, you quit. And that limits your potential loss. In other words, if you fail, you fail fast. That frees up resources—both time and money—to try a second venture.

And even if you start a new venture and get to the end point—defined as reaching the limits of what you were prepared to lose—the decision to quit isn't fatal, since you didn't risk more than you could afford. It is simply time to regroup and think about what you want to do next.

Contrast that to what happens if you employ Prediction. You plan seemingly forever. You assemble a team, which takes time. If you go the traditional funding route and look for venture capital money, it can take as long as two years (really) to get the money you need—if they decide to fund you, and they probably won't. Venture capitalists fund about 1,200 out of the 600,000 new businesses started every year. Of those 600,000, the U.S. Small Business Administration says 66% survive two years, and other research shows 44% survive eight years.

Do the math. In that same two years, you might start and fail in two ventures and start a third, and have a good chance of owning 100% of a successful firm, as contrasted with a .2% chance of owning part of a venture capitalist–funded firm.

In the worst of all possible worlds, you are going to fail quickly and cheaply as a result of using CreAction. That is not a bad thing.

And while you are spending all this time, the marketplace is changing and your window of opportunity may have closed.

Limiting the downside is almost always good

As you have seen, employing the concept of affordable loss does two things: on the one hand, if you fail, it keeps your failures small. By definition, you never lose more than you can afford to. On the other hand, it gives you a different way to evaluate an opportunity, a way that does not depend entirely on profits.

You entered into a new venture for some reason. It could be to make a lot of money, but it could be because "I can't stand my boss; I'm going off on my own." You might do it because of a noble aim: "I really wanted to help women back home," or it could just be that "if I don't start my own company now, I never will." Using affordable loss frees you to use other motivations than generating the highest return on assets (although as we said, "I want to make a lot of money" is a more than acceptable reason for starting a business). But although the reason for starting a business can be open-ended, the amount of money at risk is clearly defined—it is limited by how much you can afford to lose.

AFFORDABLE LOSS AND
CAPITAL-INTENSIVE IDEAS

Here's a question we get a lot:

"But what if I need $250 million [or some other huge number] to get my venture off the ground? Does the concept of affordable loss work here as well?"

The short answer is: "Sort of."

The longer answer is: "Not really. (And that's not a bad thing.)"

Let us explain both answers.

Clearly, you can use all the principles of affordable loss to help you determine if you are truly committed to starting your manufacturing facility, biotech lab, or whatever the venture is that will consume a lot of capital. But at some point, you are going to need to attract serious money to make it happen. And that will mean finding serious investors, investors who are going to rely—and will want you to rely—on Prediction.

That's perfectly fine. Remember what we have said from the beginning. CreAction—and "affordable loss" is part of CreAction—isn't designed to replace Prediction. There are still going to be places—such as raising huge amounts of capital—where Prediction, with its emphasis on future cash flows and return on investment, will, and should, dominate. This is one of those places, so predict away.

One more thing about this. Those investors you are asking for huge bucks are going to looking to your background to see if you have ever started something successfully. As we have seen, the fastest way to get a new venture up and going is by using CreAction. So, if you don't have a success under your belt, you may want to use CreAction to help you obtain one (or two) before you go searching for the big bucks.

It is a very useful exercise.

Takeaways from Chapter 7

1 | **Know how much you are willing to risk** before getting underway.

2 | **Try to not lose that much** (or anything at all).

3 | **Walk away when you don't succeed**, or when you become convinced you cannot succeed for technical, market, or personal reasons (such as you will exceed your affordable loss).

Bring other people along

(acquiring self-selected, committed stakeholders). Having a large pool of people who can help make your vision come true is a wonderful resource. That's why you want to view everyone as a potential customer or collaborator (but only the committed get to vote!). Here's how to enroll people in your idea, and what to do with them once you have them on board.

People who want to dismiss CreAction out of hand, for whatever reason, tend to say: "This is nothing more than ready, aim, fire."

But the real summary is: "Aim. Fire." There's not a lot of getting ready.

At its heart, what we have been saying in the first seven chapters is: When you are in a situation where you don't know what is going to happen next, and the cost of acting (to find out) is low, then fire with what is at hand, or what can be assembled quickly.

We have seen throughout that serial entrepreneurs, who as you will remember are people who have started more than one successful company and who are wonderful at using CreAction, usually don't spend a lot of time doing traditional research. They prefer to discover if there is a market/audience for what they want to do by going out and asking people if they want to buy.

They certainly don't do a lot of competitive analysis. In one study, some 74% of them reported they were not concerned with competitors, or that they consider potential competitors irrelevant until they know if there is a market for their idea.

But one place where they say they spend a lot of time—and urge you too as well, whether you are starting a new company or organizing a community initiative—is in trying to get as many committed people as they can to enroll in their efforts early on. Having self-selected, committed stakeholders join you is a way to spread the risk, confirm that you have a worthwhile idea, obtain additional resources, and have more fun. In fact, serial entrepreneurs told Saras that they believed that **the growth of their potential enterprise was limited only by the number of collaborators they could attract, not by how much money they could raise**.

Instead of being worried about being attacked from the outside by competitors, people who employ CreAction try to strengthen their base. One way to do that? Attract committed stakeholders who share your vision. (You can and should do this even if you're not creating a business.)

Because this is such a big idea, it is worth spending some time exploring it. First, we'll put what we are going to be discussing in context. Then we'll give you a proven approach so that you can enroll others yourself.

Part I: Tangible exchanges

If you're starting a business, the thing you want most is sales. Serial entrepreneurs passionately believe that. They start selling as soon as they can. Maybe they have a prototype. Maybe it's only a specification sheet. They simply don't wait for a polished product unless they have to.

This is still good advice if you're not starting a business. You want to start exchanging tangible things as soon as you can. Getting into the market early (to see if there is a "buyer" for your idea or someone who shares your desire) lowers your cost and spreads the risk. Moreover, having a potential buyer (consumer/partner) tells you that they like your idea and confirms that you're on a good track. It builds your confidence and credibility with others (which is an asset).

As we discussed in Chapter 5, when you are thinking of starting something new, you want to do an inventory of your assets, which includes, among other things, asking yourself: "Who am I; what do I know; and who do I know?" Attracting self-committed stakeholders clearly falls into the "who do I know" category; it is another way of expanding the means you have at your disposal.

Many of us have aspirations that exceed the assets we have at hand. By adding self-committed stakeholders, you are accumulating additional resources. The knowledge network and assets these people have can be added to your own. That's no small thing, since very few of us have the wherewithal and/or abilities to start something completely from scratch.

Of course, some people prefer to go it alone. A friend of ours in the construction business started as a framer and bootstrapped himself to the point where he is now constantly building six new homes at a time. He is worth millions, and he owns 100% of his business. He took an extremely long time to get to this point, because he financed everything himself. He was willing to take 100% of the risk in exchange for 100% of the gains.

The committed stakeholders who join you will help change your original idea—if they're brought in early enough in the process. They end up being collaborators and taking ownership of what is created. They become, in the very real sense of the word, co-creators. The initial vision becomes shared, it expands, and it becomes "ours" instead of just yours.

As you scale up, you end up bargaining and negotiating with the people who join (this is not a bad thing; they are smart and have good ideas), and as a result move from "me" to "we." As in, "we want to do this going forward," as opposed to "this is what I want to do."

As a result of this addition, the process you will go through in creating something new will look like this:

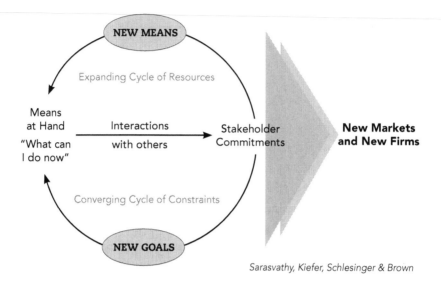

Sarasvathy, Kiefer, Schlesinger & Brown

As you get these committed stakeholders to join, their inputs and suggestions should be taken into account without regard to *possible* stakeholders who may or may not join later. In other words, the people who are there **today** determine the course of the venture. If that alienates people who come along later and say, "I would have joined, but because you did X yesterday, I won't," so be it. You are operating in the here and now.

Interactions with other people who make commitments yield new means and in many cases new goals. And this process iterates on and on as you keep adding self-committed stakeholders.

And, of course, the people who are involved with you employ their own understanding of affordable loss to decide how much they are willing to risk in your venture. You need to keep that in mind. While it is certainly possible that they will contribute significant amounts of assets (money, time, contacts) to your venture, the odds are that their investment will be far less than yours. Like you, they are going to contribute according to what they want and can afford, and your venture may not be the most important thing going on in their life.

Can there be a problem with having too many stakeholders involved? Absolutely. If they are the ones with the money, they could try to take you in a different direction than you want to go. ("I know you want to do X, but I am only going to provide the money if you modify X [so that it is something different].") And all those competing voices, ideas, and personalities can make moving forward a whole lot like herding cats. Either you learn to manage this situation—there are entire books on the subject—or you decide to do something else.

If you fail, it won't hurt as badly

Taking on committed stakeholders may or may not decrease the chances of failure as you try to get your new venture under way, but it does reduce both the expense (since you are spreading the risk across an increased number of people/resources), and the time you need to invest. (If you manage the process correctly, having more people involved allows you to move faster.)

What that means is should you strike out, the failure will occur earlier and at less cost. This has three positive implications:

1. You'll get more times at bat.

2. You won't deplete your resources as fast.

3. Because of one and two, you will get to explore other opportunities that may be better suited for you. (The failure taught you both what won't work, and what you didn't like.)

All of these are good things. To make sure you achieve the maximum benefit of adding committed stakeholders, keep these thoughts in mind:

• Focus on current reality and what's immediately actionable, not what could happen (a long-term plan).

Your immediate goal should be taking the next smart step toward what you want to accomplish.

- Everyone is a potential stakeholder until proven otherwise (by saying no), but only people who commit get a say in shaping the outcome. Others just get an opinion.

- Everyone commits only to what he/she wants and can afford to lose, not what is calculated to reach goals. If someone has committed $1,000 to help you, but you need $5,000, don't browbeat them into providing the additional $4,000. Find it elsewhere. Affordable loss for others is different than it is for you. Accept that and move on.

- The result of the endeavor is determined by actual commitments and negotiations, not pre-determined goals.

- As more commitments are made, goals become constrained and solidified to the eventual point that new members must (more or less) take the idea as they find it or forgo membership. At some point, it becomes too late to dramatically alter the product/service/idea being considered.

Part II: Intangible exchanges

By now the idea of obtaining additional self-selected, committed stakeholders probably appeals to you, so let's turn our attention to how you gain the commitment of others. For this, we need to look at something that, while related and often comingled (and confused with) selling, is quite different. We're talking about enrollment. It's not getting somebody to do something that you want them to do. It's enabling them *to put their own name on the roll*.

The simple fact is that the only one who can get you to commit to anything is you. And that's true for everyone else as well.

There are three questions you might have at this point about enrollment:

1. *Where should I begin?* (The answer is: with you. You need to enroll yourself.)

2. *As I start to reach out to people, what should I keep in mind?* (The answer: You want to create an authentic relationship. The only way to do this is to be completely honest with yourself and everyone you come into contact with. We know this may sound hard to believe, but we will explain why this authenticity is absolutely necessary later in the chapter.)

3. *Once that relationship is in place, then what?* (Answer: You want to be ready to offer them a course of action they can take to help you—and themselves—accomplish what they want.)

Dealing in detail with these three questions and answers will make up the road map for how this chapter will unfold.

Let's begin at the beginning.

Where do you begin?
Step #1: Be enrolled yourself

You can't expect to gain the commitment of others if you're not committed yourself. You must *want* to make your idea a reality. Starting anything new is hard enough if you are committed. If you are not, you are going to be easily distracted and won't have an overwhelming desire to follow through. Both of those things can be fatal to success. Others can sense if you are not enrolled. They can tell you are not excited about the idea or truly committed to making it happen. And if they get that feeling, they are bound to ask: "If he is not really into it, why should I be?"

If you try to enroll someone when you are not truly enrolled yourself, you end up selling. As we will see, that is a far different thing.

Step #2: A relationship of authenticity with a person who cares. (Honesty really is the best policy.)

Okay, you are truly committed to the idea. Now you want to get people to come along. What's the next step?

You start talking to anyone and everyone about what you want to do. And you are genuine and transparent, because you want an authentic relationship. So, not only do you tell them the positive and negatives, to the extent you know them, you also tell them why your idea is so important to you. If it is because you want to make a lot of money, tell them. If it really is all about saving the whales, say that. Remember, one of the results in enrolling people is a lasting relationship. You can only build a meaningful relationship if you are being completely honest.

As we said, people who enroll in what you are doing should be inspired to take action. And one of the first actions you want them to take is to tell you what they think of your idea. If you're sitting there talking to someone about what is really important to you, it is the most natural thing in the world to want to know if what you are excited about rings their chimes; you want to know if it did anything for them. You want to hear something back!

If the response is negative, or not what you hoped, that's fine. All that means is you are at a dead end (at least as far as the enrollment process goes with this person). Far better you should know that early on. What you don't want to do is to continue to expect enrollment when it is clear it doesn't make sense for this individual.

By contrast, when you have your sales hat on, and you *will* need to put your sales hat on, you need to get the potential customer to buy. That is your objective. But there's nothing you can do to "get someone to enroll." When you try, you'll invariably become manipulative and start selling your vision. The person you are trying to sell to will see right through it. People can immediately sniff out when you are trying to get them to do something, even if it is in their best interest. There is no reason to go down this road when what you are looking for is genuine commitment to your cause. People either want to enroll or they don't.

Let's suppose the person you are talking to gets excited. Well, this, of course, is a good thing, but not necessarily helpful. They may be excited *for you*. They may be happy that *you* have found something that feels right *for you*. But it *does not mean that they are willing to join you*. It's only when what you have talked about is exciting to them personally that they will want to enroll. The deeper the connection between what you are talking about and what is important to them, the more likely they are to put their shoulder to your wheel alongside you. And, fortunately, that happens fairly frequently. When it does, you end up discussing what is important to both of you. At that point, your vision clarifies *to you* and actually changes, even if only a bit, to become *our vision*. (For a terrific example of how one organization handles the issue of enrollment, see the discussion of Willow Creek below.)

FINDING (AND ENROLLING) BELIEVERS

You have found some people who seem to believe in your mission and who you think could be valuable stakeholders. How do you get them from "well, that is an interesting idea," to "I really want to be a part of what you want to do"?

How do you get them to enroll and become part of your team? When you put it that way, it sounds an awful lot like a religious conversion.

Since that is the case, let's take a look at how the pros do it. Perhaps no one deals with the issue of enrollment (conversion) better than the Willow Creek Community Church, a non-denominational, evangelical Christian megachurch. Some 23,000 people attend one of its three services every weekend, and Willow Creek excels at converting casual believers into devoted followers of Jesus Christ.

How? Not by proselytizing. The church, just like successful serial entrepreneurs, believes that conversion can only come if you enroll someone in your mission. And the first step in that enrollment is to form a relationship of authenticity with the person you are trying to get to come along.

So from the beginning, the church rejected the notion that you could somehow to get someone to enroll through electronic means (a video, TV show, or website) or written ones (a book or pamphlet). Conversion to a belief in Jesus Christ can only come, they say, through having an authentic relationship with someone who cares—i.e., someone who is truly enrolled themselves—in this case someone who is already a member of the Willow Creek church.

And how does the church member form that authentic relationship with a non-churchgoer? The first step has absolutely nothing to do with the church itself. You and a member of the church might meet and become friendly. If you got around to talking about religion, as friends sometimes do, they would explain what their church teaches.

If you expressed an interest, they would invite you to a Willow Creek service, which is designed—in part—to negate all the traditional objections people have to going to church. It takes up too much time on a Sunday? Services at Willow Creek last 55 minutes. Churches can be foreboding places? Well, Willow Creek is on a beautiful campus, and the church itself is more like a theater than anything else, with no religious symbols anywhere. During the service there is music and entertainment, and the sermon is practical and doesn't involve guilt.

And your friend would be very clear with you up front. Not only would no one ask you for a monetary offering, they would refuse it if you offered one.

Given that the affordable loss was small—an hour or so of your time—you might attend a service or two. If you did, you'd be given time and space to process what you heard. You'd either return of your own volition or not. If you concluded "this is not for me," your new friend would remain your friend, but would ease off trying to get you to be a member of Willow Creek. Just like an entrepreneur who is "turned down" by someone they were trying to enroll, they would just look for someone else to enroll while still maintaining their relationship with you.

But, if you expressed an interest in joining the church, they would offer to enroll you in the next step in the process, which is to attend mid-week worship where biblical teaching occurs and the sacrament of Communion is served. You never progress more than one step at a time, and you enroll yourself each time. There is no sales pressure. After attending services for a while, you would be invited to join a small group of worshippers who meet to talk about their spiritual lives. And if you were comfortable with being part of a group, you would be asked to begin serving the church with your "special gift" (if you were a plumber, you might help with maintenance; technology people could help with the computer system). Only after all this would you be asked to financially contribute.

Whatever your religious orientation, we hope you can appreciate the principles employed that are so effective:

1. The people who were trying to enroll you were enrolled themselves. They truly believed in the mission of the church.

2. That enrolled person, a Willow Creek parishioner, was trying to forge an authentic relationship with you. If they did, great. If they didn't, that was fine too. They only wanted you to enroll if that was what you desired.

3. If you were prepared to move ahead, they were ready to offer an opportunity to take action, whether it was to attend a service or ultimately join the church as a member.

Step #3: Offer action

You will notice that an integral part of the enrollment process is immediately offering the person who wants to join you a role to play. There aren't open-ended commitments, such as "I will get back to you." That is the equivalent of thinking, not doing. As we said, there are many roles in enrollment, and you can propose a big part or a small one—depending on their needs and yours. But there does need to be an immediate offer so that you can take action together. When that action occurs, that's when you know the enrollment has really taken place.

THERE ARE MANY ROLES IN ENROLLMENT

Let's pause here to state what is probably obvious. There are many different ways for people to become involved when they enroll with you. Sure, they may join your venture whole hog and make it the most important thing in their life. Conversely, they may contribute every once in a while, or fall somewhere in between.

Looking for an analogy? Think election campaigns. Some people just stick a sign for the candidate on their front lawn. Others stuff envelopes, while the more committed might go door-to-door, or take time off and volunteer at the local campaign headquarters.

Each and every person is needed and should be welcomed.

The difference between selling and enrollment (and, by the way, you want both)

If you are selling, you are trying to persuade, convince, influence, sway—whatever word you want to use—someone to do something *you* want them to do. Honest selling is a noble profession. Great salespeople can make your life easier when you are looking to buy. But while a great salesperson wants you to be happy, her ultimate focus is in getting you to do what she wants: buying. Her goal is to make the sale, a transaction of real things (her goods or services for your money).

In contrast, if you are able to get someone to enroll, you have inspired them to act in favor of what *they* want to do. It is an exchange of intangibles. You can't buy anybody's commitment. You can buy their product—and they can buy yours (and again, that is perfectly legitimate)—but you can't buy commitment. They become part of your efforts because they are excited by your dream and want to become part of your efforts as a result.

That's the key distinction between enrollment and selling. Ultimately you want both. Sales without enrollment yields a customer. And that is good, but perhaps a missed opportunity. (They might have spread the word about you.) Enrollment without a sale creates ambassadors. That's good, too. But could you have "taken their order" as well? When you have enrollment with sales—as we will see later in the chapter when we talk about the shopping channel QVC—you have a home run.

If we were to present the differences in the form of a table, it would look like this:

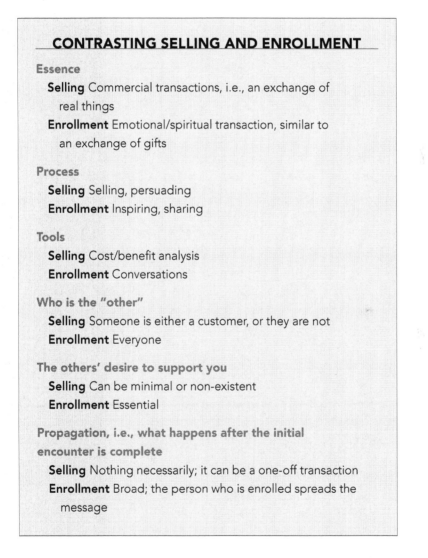

CONTRASTING SELLING AND ENROLLMENT

Essence
   Selling Commercial transactions, i.e., an exchange of real things
   Enrollment Emotional/spiritual transaction, similar to an exchange of gifts

Process
   Selling Selling, persuading
   Enrollment Inspiring, sharing

Tools
   Selling Cost/benefit analysis
   Enrollment Conversations

Who is the "other"
   Selling Someone is either a customer, or they are not
   Enrollment Everyone

The others' desire to support you
   Selling Can be minimal or non-existent
   Enrollment Essential

Propagation, i.e., what happens after the initial encounter is complete
   Selling Nothing necessarily; it can be a one-off transaction
   Enrollment Broad; the person who is enrolled spreads the message

SALES AND ENROLLMENT

A terrific example of what can happen when enrollment and sales come together involves an unlikely source: QVC, the online shopping channel. You know the place. It's where the on-air "talent" tries to sell you merchandise.

The hosts are not scripted, because the network wants the sales pitches to be as friendly and authentic as possible. By way of preparation, the network puts the presenter in a room where they get to play with the merchandise; they are given the demographics of who it is likely to appeal to, and then they're asked to figure out a way to sell it. One of the most effective salespeople, bar none, was a former high school Spanish teacher, Kathy. One story will make the point.

QVC had failed miserably when it first tried to sell computers, back when personal computers were just being introduced. Like everyone else, they had tried to sell computers on the basis of capabilities—bits and bytes, storage, and the like. And unless you truly understood how the machines worked—and let's face it, most of us didn't, and still don't—no one was going to plunk down $2,100 for a machine based on its specs.

Kathy took a different approach. At the beginning of her hour, she walked onto the set with a sealed box. Inside, she said, contained exactly the same computer you would receive if you ordered. She more or less said, "I am your friend, Kathy. I'm going to spend the next half hour showing you the process I went through that convinced me that this is one of the most valuable tools you can ever have in your life."

As she began talking, a man walked onstage and began to take the computer out of the box. She introduced him and said, "Steve is going to put the computer together while we talk. You can see it really isn't any harder than plugging the power cord into the socket, plugging the mouse into the computer—you just push it in—and plugging in the monitor. It took me more time to get the computer out of the box than it did for me to get it up and running."

And then Kathy began discussing the product. She started by saying, "I know nothing about computers. I haven't a clue how they work. All I know is there is this whole world of things we can do, and we just have to get over that first hump of actually having a computer."

She has this thing beautifully timed. She talks about what computers can do, stopping everyone once in a while to talk to Steve to underscore how simple the set up is, and at the 27-minute mark you have a computer that's booted up and fully functioning, and the camera zooms in so you watch her surfing the QVC website.

Her viewers said, "Wow, Kathy just did this. I can do this." In the next half hour, Kathy basically reviewed what she had done, and by the time the hour was up, QVC had sold millions of dollars worth of computers with virtually no returns. That was millions in sales simply by creating a fundamental relationship of authenticity coupled with selling. She was authentic. She talked about how she was a novice. And she showed every step in the process.

YOU MUST REMEMBER THIS
Takeaways from Chapter 8

1 **Enrollment is getting people to buy in** and be excited with you. It's a voluntary, personal commitment on their part.

2 **Selling** is getting someone else to do something that *you* would like them to do.

3 **You want both.** Sales without enrollment is a customer, and that's fine. Enrollment without a sale creates people who talk positively about what you are trying to do. That's good too. But when you have both, à la Kathy at QVC, truly remarkable things happen.

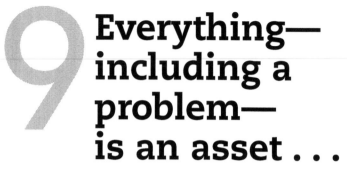

Everything— including a problem— is an asset . . .

if it is handled correctly.

We aren't big on clichés. In a world of limited resources, the idea of "win-wins" doesn't happen often. "Giving 110%" is just, well, "fuzzy math," and as for "we have to push the envelope," have you ever actually tried to push an envelope? It's a lot like "pushing string."

However, there is one much overused phrase we do think has merit: "There are no such things as problems; just opportunities."

CreAction is based, in part, on that assertion.

In the Prediction world we grew up in, we were taught either to avoid the unexpected, or to overcome it. It's all about efficiency. Optimizing. Achieving the objective quickly with as few deviations as possible. That's understandable in the Prediction universe. You have spent all this time figuring out what is going to happen (predicting) and now it is all about making that prediction a reality. So, not surprisingly, people get upset when something unexpected appears in their path. The deviation from the plan needs to be eliminated or overcome as quickly as possible.

However, CreAction is all about exploiting the contingencies and leveraging the uncertainty by treating unexpected events as an opportunity to exercise control over the emerging situation. Those who are successful in starting companies, or creating anything new for that matter, learn not only to work with the surprise factor, but also to take advantage of it.

Because people who use CreAction often begin with a very loose notion of their goals ("I want to find a job in the entertainment industry"), they can incorporate what they learn from the problems/obstacles they encounter along the way. ("Hmm. I thought there would be a chance to open my own nightclub that could feature cutting-edge bands. But that market is already sewn up in the place where I want to live. That's just the current reality I face. Maybe I can either figure out a way to work with those clubs—I could serve as a talent scout—or take advantage of the work they have already done. I could create a magazine that writes about the new music scene and get the clubs to advertise."

ANOTHER REASON THIS ALL SOUNDS SO FAMILIAR

If you think about it, incorporating the obstacles/opportunities in our path is how most of us stumbled into our careers. While there were some people who knew they were going to be firefighters, doctors, or accountants from an early age, the rest of us took an entry-level job in a field we (sort of) liked, and our careers evolved from there. If you ask someone in their 50s if they could ever have imagined back in high school that this is the way they would be earning their living, we bet you that 85% of them would say "heck no."

In most contingency plans, surprises are bad; the "what if?" scenarios are usually worst-case ones. But people who employ

CreAction do not tie themselves to any theorized or preconceived market, strategic universe, or set path for making their idea a reality. For them, problems are a potential resource as opposed to a disadvantage. ("Who knew I would end up starting a magazine supported by the very clubs that I thought would be my competitors?")

Problems are good news (almost always). Honest.

They very often do something with the things that surprise them, treating those surprises as a gift (see below). To understand why that is true, and also to better understand why obstacles can be a good thing, we need to take a step back.

OBSTACLES WELCOME

Everything is a gift.

Well, maybe not every single thing imaginable, but assuming that everything *is* a gift is a good way of looking at the problems/surprises you'll encounter in getting a new venture off the ground.

Why should you react to a problem with gratitude, whether you are trying to start a business or create anything else? There are a number of reasons. First, you were going to find out eventually what people did and did not like about your idea. Better to learn it now before you sink more resources into the venture.

And as we have discussed, that feedback could help you take your product/service in another direction, or serve as a barrier to your competitors.

The same holds true if you were surprised. Why were you surprised? By definition, you were probably predicting/expecting something else. But as we talk about in Chapter 6, Action Trumps Thinking—until you act you never really know if something you think will work actually will. Here, you acted and got evidence. True, it was not what you were expecting or even wanted, but, as we have pointed out, that still puts you ahead of

---

the person who is employing Prediction. They are still predicting, and not acting. *Thus, they don't have evidence.* All they have is what they think may be true. In contrast, you know something they don't (yet), and that is an asset.

Bad news

Okay, so it's not a surprise. It's a disappointment. No reasonable person can define what you've encountered as anything but a problem. Most people will try to solve it and get rid of it. That's fine if you can. The problem has gone away and, again, you've learned something that others might not know.

But what if you can't solve it? Accept the situation to the point of embracing it. Take as a given that it won't ever change, and turn it into an asset. What can you do with the "fact" that it won't ever change? Maybe it presents a heretofore unseen opportunity. Maybe you build it into your product or service in a way that no competitor (having not acted) could imagine. Instead of resisting and lamenting it, treat it as a gift *and turn it to your advantage*, something that the competition won't have, something that will serve as a protectable barrier to entry, if only for a while.

The thing to remember is this: Entrepreneurs, and people who think like entrepreneurs, work with what they have at hand—whatever comes along. They try to use everything at their disposal. And that is why they are grateful for surprises, obstacles, and even disappointments. It gives them more information and resources to draw upon.

How the world works

Remember one of the central tenets of CreAction: Action Trumps Thinking. (See Chapter 6.) One of the key reasons it does is you never know for sure that your reasoning is correct until you take action to discover if you are right. You may *think* you know how the market will react, or whether you can find a customer for your product or people who will support your new nonprofit idea, but until you actually do something to find out, you'll never know for sure.

But what this means is that every step you take in the journey could change where you decide to end up.

You are only one thought away from an insight that can make a problem go away, perhaps turning it into an opportunity in the process.

Here's why. Every action you take causes a change in reality. (Thinking doesn't.) You thought you would be able to sell 100 widgets a day, but it turns out the market reacted by buying 200 (or 50). You then have to stop and re ect on the reaction your action caused and see what you have learned from selling more (or less) than you expected. You are no longer speculating about what might happen. You know, and you have to figure out what it means and what you are going to do next.

How do you get creative with a surprise? Well, if the surprise is a good one, you take full advantage of it. For example, you thought the world would love your new iPhone accessory. But you have been overwhelmed by demand.

The logical thing to do is to ramp up production, add distributors (perhaps worldwide), and think about creating additional products not only for the iPhone but for all other smartphones like BlackBerries. You would pursue this path until it no longer felt right (it was taking up too much time; you realized you never wanted to run a company, only start one, or whatever). At that point, you might sell what you have and do something else.

If that surprise was a negative one—i.e., your actions did not go as you thought they would; you encountered a problem or even a setback—it is then time to figure out a way of using that negative to your benefit. Problems and even setbacks are resources to be employed to your advantage. We'll explain.

Problems = Advantage

Running headlong into a problem and then solving it can give you a barrier to competition, or at least a remarkable head start in the marketplace. Why? Because you acted, and the competition didn't.

As a result, you know something they don't.

Isadore Sharp, founder of the extremely upscale Four Seasons hotel chain, serves as a case in point. When he started out, he assumed that the only thing that would matter for him was to be in the best locations. The problem he ran into was that every other hotel chain had the same idea. That was a huge negative surprise. If you are doing what everyone else is, you don't have an advantage.

In solving that problem, he stumbled on what turned out to be the Four Seasons' ultimate competitive advantage. He created a two-pronged barrier to entry, as he explains in his autobiography, *Four Seasons: The Story of a Business Philosophy*.

"One was our inventory of hotels . . . the largest group of authentically first-class hotels in the world, a physical product no other company had to the same degree. . ." The advantage was that he could offer the frequent traveler who wanted luxury one-stop shopping when it came to staying in any of the world's major cities.

The other advantage was his people. "Three decades ago, we had decided that what our customers most desired was whatever would make time away from home most pleasurable and productive, so we set about raising service levels to match our first-class decor, an historic judgment call that had made superior service the major determinant of hotel profitability and competitiveness, and while finally recognized now by every hotel company in the world, we had a long head start, so that all our staff in all our hotels were service-oriented, and every employee was focused on delivering service no other company could match."

According to Sharp, "Location was no longer foremost in getting and keeping customers, it was people, people, people. This was now the decisive factor in our two-fold barrier to entry."

That negative surprise you encounter can ultimately become a barrier to competition, if you treat it as a gift as Sharp did. He accepted the problem that what he thought was going to be an advantage—location—wasn't. (Everyone else could build in the same place.) He then took that fact (we have terrific locations, but many other people do too) and asked what he could do with that. His conclusion: We can provide excellent service at these superior locations. That has given him a terrific edge in the marketplace.

<hr/>

TO HELP WITH YOUR THINKING

Take a piece of paper and draw a vertical line down the middle.

On the left side make a list of obstacles you are facing, things that are keeping you from achieving what you want. It can be one thing or many. They don't have to be major problems like creating world peace or figuring out a way to found a $1 billion company that you can start in the next 20 minutes. (They can be, though.)

Then spend five minutes figuring out as many ways as possible to solve them, and write those solutions on the right side.

When you are done, show your list of problems (and potential solutions) to someone else and have them help build on your solutions.

Once that is done, spend an extra five minutes together trying to turn those problems and solutions into an opportunity.

Here's one way the exercise could play out. Your problem is you have a hard time waking up in the morning. Your solution: multiple alarm clocks placed all around the bedroom, so you have to physically get out of bed to turn them off.

Your friend takes the idea further by suggesting that the clocks be set to go off one minute apart (7:00, 7:01, 7:02), so you have to get up and stay up. And she suggests as further back up that you arrange for a friend to call you at 7:15 each morning.

That triggers the thought that might allow you to move from solving the problem to creating an opportunity: Could you create a business around waking people up? (Not only providing wake-up calls like they do in hotels, but delivering breakfast and the morning papers as well.)

Taking that extra step of turning a solution to a problem into a potential profitable opportunity is what CreAction is all about.

Coming full circle

We began the chapter talking about business clichés. Let's end the same way. The takeaway from this chapter is clear. If you come across lemons—otherwise known as business problems/obstacles—do indeed make lemonade.

Try this approach next time you encounter something unexpected. Despite how unpleasant it seems, say, "This is really good news," and then try to make it so. The heart of CreAction is the ability to turn the unexpected into the profitable. That means your default position should be that there is never a problem without a potential profitable/pleasant solution lurking somewhere.

The understanding that a) not all surprises are bad, and b) surprises, whether good or bad, can be used to create something new, is a central part of CreAction. The key is to do something positive with those surprises.

TO HELP WITH YOUR THINKING II

It can be difficult to find solutions to the problems that you encounter or to the things that have you stuck. One reason it is so hard is because you are the person trying to solve the challenge at hand. You see things a certain way. And the problem with that, as Einstein is said to have observed, is "problems cannot be solved by the same level of thinking that created them."

To escape that quandary, sit down with someone, describe your problem, and then say to the person you're with, "Tell me five ways this could be an asset for me."

If you do—and listen with an open mind to what they have to say—three things might happen, all of them good:

- Simply explaining the problem out loud could give you an insight into solving it.

- Your friend might actually come up with a solution.

- Even if she doesn't, her suggestions could spark new thinking on your part.

Takeaways from Chapter 9

1 | **If you are faced with a pleasant surprise**, for example more people liked your idea than you could have ever imagined, simply proceed down the path you were heading—although you might want to move a bit faster to make sure the opportunity window doesn't close.

2 | **If it is an unpleasant surprise**, treat it as a gift. It gives you new information, new evidence, that your competition does not have. Accept it wholeheartedly.

3 | **If you can't**, see if it points to an opportunity.

4. | **If it doesn't**, make it an asset.

10 An extremely short introduction to using CreAction "everywhere else"

and an explanation of the two roles you are going to play when you do. (Our transition into the final third of the book.)

The focus up until now has been on *you*, making sure *you* understand the logic that governs CreAction and how *you* can use it in beginning your new venture.

But as we have shown throughout, starting a new business is not the only place you can apply CreAction. There is a reason we used the subtitle "*creating what you want in an uncertain world.*" We included the word "world" because the same approach, principles, and logic that will help you start a new venture can also be used everywhere else.

And to prove it, we have invented a surrogate for you and your life: Susan Smith. Susie, as we have come to think of her, is pretty typical. She works at MegaGalactic, Inc., an international conglomerate based in the U.S. She is married to Dan, who, as it turns out, is thinking of finally starting that company that he has always dreamed of. They have two kids: Becky, 14, and Scott, 11, and Susie is active both in the community (she serves as the parent representative to the school board in Gladstone, Missouri) and in her church.

Using Susie as our example from here on out, we are going to talk about how everything we have discussed up until now works both:

A) Within organizations—the subject of the next chapter, and

B) When you are involved with non-work related groups: friends, family, and social and religious organizations, and within society in general.

Before we begin, some level setting about what's ahead. If you think about it, no matter where you find yourself in all the relationships we just rattled off, there is only one of two roles you could be playing. You are either:

1. An actor who is using the principles we have talked about, and the others around you don't necessarily understand what you're doing or why you're doing it (and it would be handy for you—for whatever reasons—if they did); or

2. You're part of the supporting cast. You are helping someone, or a group of someones, try to accomplish their goals.

We've come up with some general principles for each case, which will apply in all the situations we are about to discuss. Let's take them one at a time.

As an "actor"

Here, you are the person trying to get something done—helping your church (you think it would be a good idea if it worked with the women's shelter in town); getting your friends together to do something—anything—to improve your local schools; working with your family to figure out a unique way to honor your grandmother.

To have these things happen requires you to develop your own capacity to use CreAction to the fullest. This involves:

- Remembering this latent but perhaps forgotten capacity you have for CreAction; making a point to practice it on a ongoing basis in order to break the habit of overusing Prediction; and

- Developing the ability to discern when a situation is, for your purposes, unknowable and therefore ripe for CreAction.

All of this ultimately occurs re exively. It's like becoming bilingual.

If you have ever seen people—kids are the best example—who are bilingual, you will understand how this will eventually work for you. Not only do these kids instinctually speak one language in one setting (English in school) and a second somewhere else (Spanish at home), but they bounce back and forth with their friends who have the same language skills, using the Spanish word or phrase that is most evocative when it is appropriate, and English when it is better. So somebody who is uent in two languages uses both to express their ideas. One is more dominant than the other depending on the circumstances.

It should be exactly that way when it comes to the way you approach a problem: Sometimes Prediction makes sense, other times CreAction does.

When you are the actor you need to be able to explain to people, in terms they instantly understand, what you are doing and why. At least three things can help you here:

- Always have the next step you want to take be both compelling and affordable. It's easy for people to understand why you're doing something when it sounds exciting and carries little cost or risk. (As a result, they are more likely to come along or support you.)

- Ensure that you really want to take that next step. You're not going to explain your idea in a compelling manner or enroll anyone if it's not something that is really meaningful to you.

- And this, of course, brings us to enrollment. How do you explain what you're doing so that people not only understand but want to help? (See Chapter 8.)

HOW TO EXPLAIN CREACTION TO OTHERS

People tell us that sometimes they get stuck when they try to explain the logic of CreAction to someone who has never been introduced to it before.

This might help serve as a template.

"Fred, I would like to be able to create or accomplish X. Doing so would be really meaningful to me for these reasons: A, B, and C. This is why I *want* to do it. Now I can't predict right now if this is going to work. As a matter of fact, I can't even be certain of the result of the next step I'm going to take, or that I won't find something else that I want to do more. But in the situation I'm in right now, action is really much smarter than sitting on my tush. So I want to act.

"It's reasonable to act because the cost is low. And maybe you've got some ideas about me lowering it further. And it's not just me by myself. I have these other people around who want to help me.

"So, that's what I want to do. And I think you could play a big part by doing X."

As a supporter

Now let's go to the situation where you're a supporting actor, so to speak. Here, your job is really to help people take wise action. Or at the very least to not get in their way. This means at least three things:

First, you help them find out what they *want* to do. Is what they are contemplating something they care about? What kind of assets do they have to get under way? What is their next low-cost step? (Could you introduce them to someone you know?) You goal here is to help them take considered action.

Second, aid them in understanding current reality as best they can. Desire and passion can distort reality. This is a potential Achilles' heel for anyone trying to start something new. They can get so caught up in what they want to do that maybe they don't perceive current reality as clearly as they might. ("Why wouldn't the mayor want to fund my idea? It makes all the sense in the world," they tell you. "I can't imagine that raising property taxes is going to be a big deal, given what I want to do.")

Finally, reinforce CreAction behavior when you observe it. For example, point out that they seem excited about the idea (if they are), and that the risk doesn't seem all that high (if it doesn't). Reinforcing *behavior* is the fastest way to embed new thinking. So when you see a friend or a family member taking a really smart low-cost step, you can applaud and reinforce their behavior. It's probably ten times better than reinforcing their thinking.

These are the kinds of things that will be really helpful for people in any setting. Let's see how they might play out with family and friends.

11

How to use CreAction in today's organizations

Traditional companies are based on the assumption that the future is going to be very much like the past. Yet, as a quick glance at the headlines shows, the world is seemingly growing more unpredictable each day. How can you introduce CreAction into the last place on earth set up to embrace it: the contemporary organization? It isn't easy. But it can be done.

Susie Smith had a problem. She had discovered a group within her 90-person department at MegaGalactic that was using CreAction, and she didn't know what to do about it. Well, actually she did know what she wanted to do. After thinking long and hard, she decided she wanted to fully support their efforts, and the thought was scaring her death.

It didn't take long for her to remember how she found herself in this situation. Two weeks before she had discovered that the "skunk works," as she had come to think of them, had been experimenting for about six months trying to find new markets, uses, and distribution channels for the communication-switching equipment that MegaGalatic sold and that Susie was ultimately in charge of.* Her initial reaction was predictable. On the one hand,

Please note: Although this story occurs within a large commercial company, it could just as well be in a large church, public school system, or government agency.

she wanted to commend their initiative. But on the other hand, she wanted to shoot them. It was taking away from their regular jobs, and worse, they had been losing money—not a lot, but losing money nonetheless—in the process. Hitting "stretch" financial goals was hard enough without this.

You understand Susie's negative reaction, of course. It's safe to say everything about contemporary Western organizations is designed to generate predictable performance. Especially for public companies. The market grants a premium to companies with smooth earnings as opposed to volatile ones (even when the long-term average performance is the same). And so the need for consistent, unsurprising results gets incorporated into every aspect of the enterprise—the formal (and informal) structures, systems and processes, habits, norms, decision-making criteria, etc.—with the ultimate aim of achieving better shareholder value.

So it's for a good reason that Prediction is pervasive in modern organizations. In predictable (or partially predictable) environments, it works! Susie's division was living proof of that. Sales had been growing 1.5% faster than the market as a whole over the previous five years, and she had stellar performance reviews to show for it.

Susie explained that to the skunk works group—four of her favorite employees, if truth be told—and they nodded as she made the case for Prediction. But then they raised a counterargument, the one that served as their touchstone as they began experimenting, an argument that ultimately persuaded Susie once they were done.

On the surface, they conceded, everything she said about the need for consistency, solid rules of thumb, and sticking to the tried and true path seemed sound. But if you dug a little deeper, they argued, you could see that the argument for consistency is built on a fatal flaw. The inherent assumption about using Prediction—thinking and acting based on the belief that the future is going to be similar to the present and the immediate past—is that *in this case there was no reason to believe it would be.*

Just take our own industry, communications broadly defined, they said. Who would have thought 20 years ago that record stores, landline phones, fax machines, VCRs, answering machines, cameras that use film, analog TVs, pay phones, newspapers, and yellow pages would be become the buggy whips of the 21st century?

"Oh, no. They're right."

In a world which is increasingly uncertain, CreAction's premise that you are better off trying to shape the future is increasingly the tool to use, they contended.

The more Susie thought about it, the more she knew they were right. That was a couple of weeks ago. And now she had a bigger problem. As a convert, she wondered how she could help introduce CreAction, which by definition is unpredictable (after all, a fundamental tenet of CreAction is "let's try this and see what happens"; there is nothing more unpredictable than that), into an organization like MegaGalatic, which is built on the premise that anything that even hints of unpredictability needs to be wiped out.

The challenge was more than daunting, even though—à la CreAction—she was planning to start with a small step: introducing this thinking only within her department at first. But even though her scope was limited, it was extremely problematic. Not only would she be challenging the way her organization thinks, she would also have to overcome all sorts of constraints that an entrepreneur would never confront if she were off trying to do something on her own.

Scaling some very high heights: a guide for managers

Think of the sorts of questions you are always faced with if you try to introduce an idea (say for a new product or service) inside a company (or a new state-sponsored program). At the very least, you will hear:

- Will it fit with our strategy?

- Will it ultimately be big enough and profitable enough to meet our larger organizational goals?

- What about the opportunity cost—how can we afford to divert the resources of our people onto something with such unknown potential?

- What about the risks to other products or programs? Could they be cannibalized?

- Will this somehow damage our brand or public image?

Answers to all these questions require Prediction. And it's not just the formal questions and hurdles that conspire to keep CreAction from fitting comfortably within companies and other organizations—there are the informal ones as well. Think of the number of departmental approvals that are typically required before anything new can be implemented; the number of presentations; the number of adjustments, tweaks, fixes, and upgrades before any action is taken.

There's a good reason Prediction is pervasive in modern organizations: It works (when the future is knowable or at least partially so). By contrast, CreAction is rather like an experimental science whose results are evaluated in arrears.

But for organizations that instantly recoil from the idea of employing CreAction, the simple fact is that it is the best approach to use when facing an uncertain future. And whether you like it or not, you should always use the right tool for the job.

If this weren't enough, there are the informal habits, procedures, and structures. In many organizations you have to brief anybody whose area will be affected by your idea. Each of these briefings has to be prepared for and delivered (taking time away from actually doing anything), and just about everyone you brief can kill the idea—either overtly, or simply through inaction—even though most of the people you will be talking to don't have the authority to approve it. Worse, many of those people will be biased towards killing it since the consequences of whatever you are proposing are unknown (or would require resources to estimate). So the "safest" decision is to just say no.

Predictable innovation

Given these obstacles, Susie tried to see if there were some half-way measure she could introduce into MegaGalatic's way of thinking, something between Prediction and CreAction. She cast around for examples. While not every large firm has the strategic imperative to innovate entirely "outside the box," they all need to innovate, she thought. How do they do it?

Not very well, some quick research showed.

Innovation in these firms tends to be things like simple line extensions and moving into adjacent markets. The companies that did it well seemed pretty happy, in no small part because these methods yield predictability, and they like being more predictable about doing unpredictable things (like creating new products and entering new markets). And, they believed, at the very least they were avoiding making mistakes. However, Susie could not find reports of these companies being thrilled with their success beyond these simple efforts.

The conclusion? Results from innovatively thinking "outside the box" are still widely unsatisfactory among established companies.

Unknowability

That brought Susie back to the central problem. Large organizations like MegaGalatic face futures of varying knowability. On one side of the spectrum, the future is "pretty predictable," in which case all the tools we currently have give us a competitive advantage over firms that don't have the tools. At the other end, firms are facing situations that are completely unknowable, and yet they still apply the same Prediction tools despite the undeniable fact that in such settings not only are they ineffective, but employing them carries greater cost in two ways.

The first is in time and resources. Applying the wrong tool—Prediction—to a situation where it will not work simply wastes both.

Second, applying Prediction's standards of success to CreAction just doesn't make sense. Here's just one example of the disconnect that can result from using a traditional return on investment requirement.

"MegaGalatic policy is that new products must produce a 15% return on investment and generate at least $25 million in additional revenue. CreAction is unpredictable, so we'd better require a 25% return and at least $50 million in sales. Hmmm, now that I think about it, I am not sure that even that's enough. Let's add a safety margin and makes sure it exceeds 30%."

Eventually, you get to the point where the hurdle rate is so high that the idea—no matter how promising—is never going to be approved.

The takeaway? A thinking process that is logical, rational, and a smart thing to do in a predictable universe gets unconsciously and habitually carried over and applied in an area where things are unpredictable. Not surprisingly, the results are far from ideal.

What do you do?

Structure

One path to introducing CreAction into large organizations is to keep it completely self-contained. In other words, you sequester your efforts to deal with, or capitalize on, the "unknowable." You can do that by creating a wholly separate organization with different rules, processes, design, etc. That was Susie's first thought. She'd send her rebel quartet to an unused warehouse across town and let them work out of there.

It is a good approach as far as it goes. You set up a little unit on the side and completely protect it from the parent.

But this has, of course, its own problems. Just to rattle off a few:

- How do you reintegrate the ideas/products/services the unit develops back into the parent company?

- Who is going to run this unit? (Obviously someone steeped in Prediction won't be a good fit, and even the most creative corporate citizens are unconsciously wedded to Prediction.)

- How will the performance of the entity be evaluated? (See our discussion earlier in the chapter about unrealistic hurdle rates.)

Scope

Closely related to the sequestered concept is limiting the employment of CreAction to certain specific activities, such as pilot projects.

But neither approach is a real, permanent solution, because the parent company itself needs to operate, at least some of the time, in the face of unknowability. You may be able to relegate certain aspects of the business landscape to a separate unit, but not all of it. Reality is not that convenient.

No, if Susie wanted to extend CreAction organization-wide, she needed to find another solution.

A learning option

So what do you need to do to make an organization hospitable to CreAction? People talk all the time about how changing an organizational culture is difficult, but embedding CreAction makes that look like a walk in the park. You aren't just changing the culture, but also the company's systems, processes, procedures, goals—the whole shebang. You just can't just "order up" this kind of thinking to permeate the entire organization (even if such an order were a good idea, which it probably is not).

Well, if that won't work, what will?

The way we classically think about organization change would argue that the way to introduce anything new is to:

1. Determine where you want to be—in this case, a company that uses CreAction when appropriate.

2. Determine how close the company is to the goal. (Answer: "Not very.")

3. Chart a course between where you want to be (a company that uses CreAction) and where you are now (one that does not).

4. Put in place rewards systems, support, and training that would allow that change to happen.

5. Add metrics that will chart the progress toward the goal, and identify when things are getting off course.

6. Do remedial work as necessary until you achieve your objective.

Sounds familiar, doesn't it? It should. It's perfect Prediction. You could go this route, but quite frankly we don't think you would like the end result very much.

First, it could take months, or maybe years.

Second, experience in organization change in virtually every setting has shown that this kind of approach is unlikely to ultimately work. While the analogy is clichéd by this point, it is also correct: Organizations, like the human body, tend to reject foreign bodies inserted into them. And, as we have seen, CreAction is about as foreign as you can get when it comes to the way established companies do their business.

Third, by going down this path, you run the risk of undermining the Prediction skills within your organization. That would be a huge mistake. Even though the universe grows seemingly more unpredictable by the minute, there is—and always will be—a huge number of things which are predictable, and you don't want to weaken or eliminate a superior skill (Prediction) that the organization has, one that is effective under the right circumstances.

Not top-down but bottom-up

Fortunately, we believe there is a way to introduce CreAction **without** replacing any of the existing structures or procedures that work well in predictable situations. It's possible, because experience has shown that *everyone is capable of entrepreneurial thought*; every one of us has the ability to operate in situations of uncertainty.

So, the secret is not to introduce CreAction from the top of the organization down—i.e., with the CEO (or superintendent or minister) saying, "from this day forward, we will add CreAction to the way the company addresses problems and opportunities"; rather, it is to have it become part of the organization from the bottom up, with individual employees—such as the skunk works group who works for Susie—using this alternative form of thinking *as the situation warrants*. (See box: *How to introduce CreAction*.)

Let's pause a moment to underscore both points. First, CreAction doesn't replace Prediction; it's an additional tool. Second, introducing it in the manner we suggest doesn't require an organization to change its existing systems. Rather, the change process begins with employees asking themselves, when confronted with a problem, "does it make sense to use CreAction in this case?"

HOW TO INTRODUCE CREACTION

We don't have a whole lot of experience introducing CreAction into large organizations. So, what we are about to suggest will likely evolve over time.

That said, from what we have seen in a variety of settings, the following approach would seem to have the greatest chance of success.

One. Instead of having the idea introduced from the top down, one or a few "early adopters" need to employ the method on their own and see if it works for them on a real project of theirs.

Two. If it does, they need to use it again and share the results with the organization's "thought leaders." These are people who are not necessarily in formal leadership positions. But they are the 5–10% of employees whose views receive a disproportionate amount of respect and attention. The power of these thought leaders is that when they have or adopt an idea, it is accepted and endorsed by the entire organization. It becomes legitimate and goes viral.

Three. Formal leaders, such as Susie, publicly support the efforts of these two groups—or at the very least allow the approach to be used.

This could be enough to increase the likelihood of CreAction taking hold and spreading organization-wide over time.

Here's an example that strikes close to home for us, which shows exactly what we are talking about.

Year in and year out, Babson College is recognized worldwide as one of the leading academic institutions when it comes to the teaching and studying of entrepreneurship. The college is also continually rated one of the best business schools in the country, and ranked as one of the world's leading executive education providers. (For example, in its 2010 rankings, Financial Times selected Babson's executive education No. 5 among top U.S. custom programs, and No. 12 among top custom programs worldwide.)

The problem for many of the students who wanted to attend, either as an undergraduate or graduate student, is that Babson only had one campus, located in suburban Boston. If you wanted to learn at Babson you needed to head to Wellesley, Massachusetts, and that was not necessarily convenient, especially if you had a full-time job elsewhere in the country.

The obvious solution? Open another campus.

The obvious concern? If Babson set up shop on the West Coast—San Francisco seemed to make sense given there are literally thousands of innovative start-ups in and around the city (Silicon Valley is within easy driving distance)—would people enroll?

Faced with that question, people who employ Prediction would argue: Let's spend $100,000 on market research to find out if there is a market for Babson on the West Coast. If there is, we can set up shop and start offering courses (something that will cost us another $100,000).

Conversely, people who employ CreAction would take a different tack. Using the let's-take-a-small-step-immediately-and-see-what-happens logic, they would say, "Why not spend $100,000 and start offering classes? If people **don't** register, then we know there is no market, and all we have lost is the $100,000 we would have spent on market research anyway. But if people attend, then a) we know there is a market and b) we will have saved $100,000 (the money we would have spent on market research)."

That's exactly what the school did. Instead of doing traditional market research, Babson in early 2010 started offering its "Fast Track MBA" (an accelerated, part-time, 24-month program designed for experienced professionals who want to advance their careers while simultaneously earning their degree). Applicants meeting the school's strict standards far exceeded expectations. Babson now has a West Coast presence.

To us this is a great example of learning how to use CreAction within a large organization (Babson in this case). The learning has to occur on two fronts—on the individual *and* organizational level.

The individual needs to say, "Instead of butting my head against the wall trying to get the organization to accept this new way of thinking, the question is how do I develop the ability to know when I should be leaning more heavily on CreAction?"

If you go this route, you need to ask yourself the following as you face any new situation: "Is this a challenge I have seen before, or one where I am likely to know what is going to happen? If it is, I need to employ the Prediction I have been trained to use for years. Or is it a situation where the future is basically unknowable? If that is the case, I need to apply CreAction."

If it is the latter, you act exactly as you would if you were on your own as an entrepreneur. You would say "okay, so this really is an exercise in knowing who I am; who I know; what I know; getting things done through my personal networks; and doing everything in a way that absolutely minimizes the cost." This is an argument for being clever and looking for innovative ways to work within the bounds of your own (and your organization's) affordable loss. That way, if someone discovers what you are doing (and the reasoning you are applying), you can point out the risk to the corporation is de minimis, while the upside could be huge.

Alone, you can't convince your company to create a new structure, but you can persuade it to perhaps attack a problem from an unusual angle. ("Hey, can we think about it a different way, boss?") That you can do, especially if what you follow up with is a way to save the company money, or operate more efficiently.

You can't change the fact that there are cubicles and an existing culture and way of doing things. But "smart is smart," and we're talking about you offering up an additional way of viewing problems. You'll never get in real trouble for doing that, especially if you do it gently by saying "can we think about this differently?"

That is the first kind of learning that has to take place to introduce CreAction into the organization. The second kind is an *organizational* learning. After the idea of CreAction has started to take hold, you need to come up with an answer to: "How do we build this capacity within our firm in a way that is consistent with our strategy?"

There is no "one size fits all" recipe for this. We're dealing with something that is essentially a creative act, and consequently each organization has to handle it in its own unique way. If the company looks to adopt somebody else's version, it's because it's leaning right back into predictive thinking: "If I imitate them somehow, it will be good for me." Imitation will probably not be very successful. Despite what they teach you in business school, no two organizations are exactly the same.

So how do you induce organizational learning about CreAction? The task is actually simpler than you might think. Encourage people to:

A. Regain their natural capacity for CreAction. This is easy. As we have seen throughout, this is the way we figured things out before we went to school.

B. Employ the use of CreAction in settings that are inhospitable to Prediction. This looks easy as well. It requires four things:

- Learn to recognize when a particular setting has a high degree of essential unknowability, and thus the use of CreAction is appropriate (and Prediction is not).

- As an alternative to "more study," develop a compelling next step with acceptably low affordable loss. (The easiest way to do that? Ask what will get you furthest in the shortest time, with the least resources at risk.)

- Develop the capacity to enroll whatever sponsors, enablers, and approvers may be required. (It is especially important to develop the ability to explain CreAction and why it is appropriate to those who are unfamiliar with it.)

- Develop the personal desire and commitment to do the three steps above.

Where we come out

In the end, whether you believe you have the ability to help CreAction take hold inside an organization really comes down to how you think about the problem—and perhaps not surprisingly, we suggest you apply CreAction.

Analyzing the question through a Prediction lens, you can complain "I don't have any lever; I can't change the reward system, and

I can't change all the bureaucratic stuff." And the answer is, "No you can't; don't even try."

But simply through the way *you* think, and getting other people to think differently, you can have an enormous impact. Over time, the organization will absorb CreAction and employ it in—and only in—appropriate circumstances.

Large organizations are skeptical about internal entrepreneurs—intrepreneurs. And for good reason. Success with this concept has been spotty. We are not taking a position on intrepreneurship. What we are trying to do is argue that large organizations need more entrepreneurial thinking, from every source possible.

YOU MUST REMEMBER THIS
Takeaways from Chapter 11

1 **Think airline advertising.** Commercials for American Airlines, Continental, Southwest, and the like almost never show you the inside of their planes. They show where the planes can take you. In the same way, you don't want to advocate for the virtues of CreAction. You want to show how the fruits of employing CreAction can benefit the company.

2 **Think bottom-up, one person at a time.** Most change starts from the top down. The boss wants something done, and so efforts are made to get it done. For CreAction to take hold, it probably needs to come from the ranks, rooted in individual initiative.

3 **Think CreAction:** Act with what you have at hand. Enroll and bringing other people along.

4 **Think small steps.** Like mules, it can take large organizations a long time to learn anything new. Don't expect overnight success in introducing a concept such as CreAction. Be prepared to take incremental steps.

5 **Don't waste your time if it's not something you care about.**

CHAPTER

12 Using CreAction with families and friends

The good news? All the rules we have talked about up to this point apply here as well. The bad news? Well, you are dealing with your family and friends. Rationality does not always carry the day, and it certainly doesn't always triumph over emotions.

We love our families.

We adore our friends.

So we say this with all the love and affection possible: Using CreAction with either group is trying, but possible.

Susie Smith and her family serve as a case in point. She is about to sit down for what she thinks is the 83rd time with her husband of 19 years to hear what she has taken to calling (affectionately) "Dan's soliloquy."

Like Hamlet, Dan is wrestling with a huge problem. It's not as big as contemplating suicide ("to be, or not to be"), but it's big nonetheless: should he leave his well-paying job and strike out on his own? Dan, who writes speeches for the chairman of MegaGalatic—Dan and Susie met at the company 20 years ago—is convinced he has spotted a potentially huge opportunity.

Companies like MegaGalatic have tons of intellectual property (IP), but they neither employ every bit of it, nor have a need to keep it proprietary forever. True, they use some of that IP to establish a competitive advantage in the marketplace, but after they do, it often lies fallow.

"It doesn't have to be that way," Dan would explain, often at length if they were out with friends. "Toyota sold its first-generation hybrid technology to the Detroit car companies, once it started working on the fourth generation of the Prius. That's exactly the sort of thing companies could do with their intellectual property. After they used whatever portion they are going to employ to increase their market share, profits, or whatever, they could turn that IP into business review articles, op-eds, white papers, books, videos, software, whatever. And I would be the perfect person to help those firms figure out what they have that could be of interest to others. Then I could develop the products—the software, white papers, etc.—that could be sold or used, in essence, as high-end marketing materials like op-eds and thought leadership pieces."

Dan has been talking about this for years. In his initial vision, he would quit MegaGalatic and go off and start this new company. Susie, thanks to her understanding of Entrepreneurial Thought and Action principles, has convinced him that:

A) Thinking about this is a waste of time. The only way to discover if the idea will work is to take a small step toward finding out and seeing what happens.

B) Taking a dramatic step, such as quitting his job, isn't necessary. He probably could do a lot of the prep work—finding companies whose IP he could mine; lining up writers, video people, and software developers who could channel the IP—on nights and weekends and during lunch.

Susie has been supportive—"I am glad to see your enthusiasm remains high; have you thought about talking to Bill Tabor over at Enormous Co.? He is now the head of all their communication efforts and is probably the entry point over there." But Dan hasn't talked about the idea for a while, so she doesn't have a clue what he is about to say as they sit at the kitchen table.

And for a first time in a long time, her husband surprises her.

"I am ready to do it," he begins with no preamble. "I've worked up prototypes of the stuff I could sell, using MegaGalatic material, so I didn't feel guilty about doing it on company time. I showed it to the CEO and he was impressed. So if this idea bombs as a free-standing company, I think I can do it internally at the very least. But I have five companies interested. I've lined up a bunch of free-lancers and production people, so we are good to go. But I need the $25,000 we have put away in our emergency fund to get everything rolling. I have to pay the freelancers a little bit to get them to start work; I need to set up an LLC, buy the domain name, and pay a web designer to help me. And I should probably have a cushion, since I am guessing the business will be cash- ow negative for a while. You know how long it takes big companies to pay their bills. Is it okay with you if I spend all that money?"

And with that question, you get to a key difference between how Entrepreneurial Thought and Action functions in business and how it works among family and friends. There are more dimensions, different emphases, more complexity, and far more nuances when you are dealing with all this outside a commercial setting.

If you are married, when it comes to affordable loss the question to ask is not "how much am I willing to lose," but "how much are **we** willing to lose."

With arm's-length business transactions, the issue of afford-able loss might be about money, time, resources, and opportunity costs. For example, "if we do X and it doesn't work, we will be out $Y and will have blown the opportunity to have done Z (the other alternative we were considering)."

Most of this is pretty transparent and not necessarily emo-tionally loaded. Money is simply a fungible commodity; it is not something that is being saved for Becky's college education, a new roof, or an emergency. Reputation is often a factor, but it is more often public reputation: "Fred is a great salesman; Fred is a lousy salesman."

Not so when you are dealing with family. There are different and potentially serious costs to the relationships you have with the people you care about. For one thing, as Dan Smith realizes, if you are in a relationship there is no such thing as your own "affordable loss." The potential loss affects your partner (and possibly your children as well). Then there is the potential loss of face with your family. How is your spouse going to feel about you if the new venture fails; will your kids think less of you if you end up spending their college fund on an idea that ames out? In the case of family, the psychosocial dynamic and potential cost is almost always enormously important.

Moreover, in an arm's-length business transaction, failures often have no long-term consequence, or at least very little. The project will succeed or be unsuccessful. The deal will get done or it won't. But it is a rare case where the decisions are of the bet-the-company variety.

Conversely, the kinds of things you do in a family situation may resonate for decades. To oversimplify, if you failed to get the Henderson account, it may hold back your career for a while. But if you were the person who repeatedly warned your father-in-law about investing in Google ("why would anyone want shares of a search engine company?") right before the company went public, and he followed your advice and put his money in an alpaca farm instead, your spouse's side of the family may stop having anything to do with you forever.

So the steps you take with family can be more permanent, and more non-recoverable. As a result, the affordable loss calculation you do is quite different. Not only may the amount of money you are prepared to lose be less (your spouse/partner may be risk averse; you may be more predisposed to play it safe, fearing the reaction of those near and dear to you should you fail).

And things aren't different when it comes to self-selected stakeholders. In a straightforward business transaction among people who know each other slightly (or not at all), you generally understand what the nature of the deal is. People are bringing obvious resources to the table, and it's pretty clear what they expect in return.

But when you are involved with family, those things can often be far less clear, and they are frequently con icted. Family members may want to support your efforts, but maybe you don't want them to—at least not too much. (Do you really want to be beholden to your mother-in-law forever for the funding that got you under way?)

As a supporter, you may find it very easy to lend emotional support, while at the same time be unable (or unwilling) to exhibit financial support. This can cause complex and complicated feelings for the actor. ("I know my sister has the money I need. Why won't she invest it in my company?")

Just the opposite might be true in another case. ("Sure, my brother lent me the money, but he did it out of guilt. He never really believed in me.") Perhaps even more important, there are often hidden strings—maybe many, many, hidden strings—attached. The self-selected crew that you're operating with here is not as neat and tidy as it is in a business setting.

Now let's address parent/child issues. When this is a factor, it is of course a very important one. Maybe all-important.

It is hard to imagine your parents *not* being part of your self-selected, committed stakeholder group in some way or another. Even if you weren't counting on them (or didn't want them to come along at all), they're going to think of themselves as involved. That's their job. So you are going to have a presence that you can't ignore. And there are a set of expectations that are biologically induced, complicated, and unavoidable. They have perhaps the most profound need to support, educate, and backstop you. You're going to get what *they* think is support whether you want it or not. And they have some real expectations around that, some of which you cannot change.

Friends

One of our favorite expressions is "friends are the family you choose." We think that's right. In the best of all worlds, your friends provide the same love, encouragement, and support that your family does. (And often in the real world, they provide those things when your family doesn't.) But because they are emotionally involved with you, the interpersonal dynamics just described will be in play here too.

Since we already pointed out the negatives, there is no reason to dwell on them here. Instead, let's talk about how taking smart steps could work effectively with your friends and the social groups you are involved with. Consider, for example, how Susie Smith and her friends were able to create an indoor basketball court in town.

Susie was on the high school basketball team, so it is not surprising that every Wednesday night when the weather was nice, you could find her playing hoops with a bunch of her female friends. While playing on someone's backyard court during late spring and summer was fine, the Midwestern fall, winter, and early spring are cold, and there was simply no place for Susie and her friends to play indoors. The local school gyms were constantly in use, and the nearest Y wasn't convenient. As a result, except when there were unexpected warm spells, there wasn't much basketball played from November through April.

Susie and her friends wanted to change that. If they followed Prediction, they would have met with the Gladstone recreation director and convinced him to lobby the town council for both the $1 million it would take to establish a recreation center, and to add $100,000 a year into the municipal budget to cover the cost of staffing and maintaining it. Municipal governments working as they do, and town budgets being as they are, they may have gotten the center right around the time that Susie's grandchildren would be working on their behind-the-back dribbles and dunks.

Having seen how CreAction had worked for Dan and her sister (see sidebar), Susie wondered if it would be effective here as well. She contacted everyone she knew and asked them to reach out to everyone they knew to spread the word that a group of neighborhood women were trying to create an indoor basketball center at little or no cost.

Q: CAN YOU USE CREACTION AS A GUIDE TO DATING?

A: APPARENTLY YOU CAN

CreAction, we discovered to our surprise, also works on an extremely personal level. Consider, for example, romance.

Susie's sister, Cyndi, divorced for two years, has gone the Prediction route when it has come to finding love these last 24 months. She has joined computer matching services, signed up with places that arrange "just lunch" dates, and spent time in the restaurants and bars identified by *Kansas City Magazine* as "the best for singles." When asked to describe the results of all this, she says, "Not great."

Having heard her sister explain how CreAction works, she has an unusual reaction: "It sounds like the perfect dating strategy."

Understanding she could start anywhere within the process, Cyndi began by defining what she wanted: "a man who is fun to be with." Another marriage was not on the immediate agenda. From there she asked the key questions:

Who am I? What traits, tastes, and inclinations do I have; how do they align with the potential guy I am searching for? Her conclusion, which she knows she is going to have to test in the (dating) marketplace, is "this should work." Having double-checked current reality, she has concluded there have to be a certain percentage of single guys who want to spend time with a woman who has no immediate expectation of marriage.

What do I know? Again, Cyndi believes her education, training, experience, and expertise make her attractive. And the question of

Who do I know has her excited. She is convinced that by telling everyone in her personal, social, and professional networks that she is going to use CreAction to find dates, her social life is going to improve.

It turns out she was right. The people in her various networks knew lots of guys who might fit her criteria, and they were happy to make introductions and supply phone numbers.

Cyndi continues to use CreAction as she follows up on all the names. She talks to each man by phone (investing just a small amount of time, so the potential [affordable] loss is low). If the conversation goes well, she will suggest coffee. If the face-to-face meeting is promising, she decides she is willing to invest more time (a dinner date, perhaps). At each step of the process she is deciding whether it's worth taking an additional step. It's the quintessential example of CreAction, and as Cyndi told us, "It is working very well for me."

We would like to thank her for (inadvertently) suggesting our next book, **Action Trumps Everything: Navigating the dating scene in an uncertain world**.

A countless number of emails were exchanged over the next few weeks—and all of them led nowhere. True, the affordable loss was small, just the time it took to read and write the emails, but it was still frustrating. Then a friend of a cousin of one of the women who played occasionally in the Wednesday night games suggested that Susie call her older brother.

"He works for Second Shawnee Federal, you know the bank chain that is downsizing? His job is to sell off all the unwanted assets. They have an old bank building about a mile away from you that I think could work as some sort of gym."

She was right, and we will condense the next nine months into two paragraphs.

The bank official said he would be happy to donate the building, just to keep the company from paying taxes on it. One of the basketball regulars, an attorney, created Hoopstar Dreams, a non-profit, to accept the gift. The women then lobbied local businesses for the loan of machinery and donation of supplies to turn the inside of the bank into a small recreation center—the donors got to display permanent ads courtside—and seemingly everyone even vaguely related to the women spent the next 36 Saturdays doing the actual labor, under the supervision of a general contractor (the husband of one of the basketball regulars).

When the building was done, the board of the nonprofit, comprising Susie and her friends, agreed to lease the building to the Gladstone recreation department for $1 a year in exchange for a promise the town would staff the building and pick up all maintenance and insurance costs. (It is far easier to get a town to commit to hiring a couple of people and pay for operating expenses than it is to get them to lay out $1 million in a single shot.)

These days, just about every Wednesday night, no matter what the weather, you can find Susie playing basketball at the Hoopstar Dreams Recreation Center.

YOU MUST REMEMBER THIS
Takeaways from Chapter 12

1 | **Yes, Entrepreneurial Thought and Action works with family and friends, but . . .** It is an extremely big "but." The "but," of course, is the emotional component. It is just silly **not** to plan for it when you are dealing with family and friends.

2 | **The affordable loss calculation is substantially different with family and friends.** This point follows the last. When you are dealing with people near and dear, you can lose a lot more than money if something goes wrong. Plan accordingly.

3 | **Remember to play both roles.** In dealing with family and friends, you can apply CreAction when you are the one trying to bring something into being (Susie wanted to have a place to play basketball in winter) and when you are supporting someone else (Susie enabled Dan's new venture).

13 How Entrepreneurial Thought and Action can make a better world

We are not being hyperbolic with the headline. And what is intriguing for those of us who think that CreAction really can help make the planet a better place is that help is starting to arrive.

Before we get to what government, business, schools, and others are doing—and what we think they should be doing to help let Entrepreneurial Thought and Action (ET&A) ourish—let's spend a minute underscoring how ET&A can naturally lead to economic and social value creation worldwide.

Up until this point, the book hasn't been a huge public policy polemic, and we are not going to start now. So, we are going to simply rattle off four key advantages ET&A has when it comes to making the world a better place.

1. **Empowerment.** Implicit in everything that we have talked about in this book is that CreAction gives you more control over your life. You are a driver, not a passenger, as you head down the highway. Being behind the wheel always gives you more control and more options.

2. **It fosters job creation.** As we saw in Chapter 4, the *Fortune* 500 have added no new jobs—when you net out layoffs and retirements—over the last 25 years. Entrepreneurs are the only ones creating jobs and allowing people to join—and remain—in the middle class.

3. **It gives us a way to attack huge social problems.** When it comes to issues like health care, the challenge can seem so daunting that most of us are tempted to throw up our hands and either say "nothing can be done" or pass the buck to our government, which, truth be told, is probably no better qualified to address it. But our approach argues for taking a number of new, small, smart steps—a pilot project here; a different way of doing things over there—to see what happens. Positive outcomes can be built upon. The point? Taking smart steps is an essential key to making the impossible possible.

4. **You get a chance to try more things.** The best thing in life is to succeed. The second best thing is to fail quickly and cheaply, learn from the experience, and quickly try something else. If CreAction had a motto, it would be: a world of small failures on the road to great successes.

A little help from our friends

We believe the principles, concepts, and ideas we have talked about really can improve our lives. But that change for the better will occur far faster if the largest institutions in society come along. And, as we said, they are starting to.

Let's take a look at what they are doing and what we would like them to do.

Government

As we write this, one of the top priorities at the federal level is making the U.S. more entrepreneurial. Entrepreneurialism is seen as the best way to grow the economy. Our government has taken its responsibility seriously and is actively trying to foster the creation of more new businesses. This is a good thing, as far as it goes.

But this book is about Entrepreneurial Thought and Action and how it can be applied in daily life. Can government cause entrepreneurial thought? The short answer is not really. And it shouldn't. It's not its role. This isn't bad news. Entrepreneurialism has flourished since the dawn of civilization. Our society is built on millennia of entrepreneurial acts. Entrepreneurial thinking is built into our genes. We will think entrepreneurially. We will act entrepreneurially with or without government. If government has a role, it is to keep things from interfering with that.

Oh, and there may be one other role government can play (a role we will touch on in a minute): helping out educators.

Business

What about our businesses? Will they foster entrepreneurial thought? We've spoken about how CreAction is counterintuitive to how large organizations reason. Yet there is reason for hope. Anything that promotes better business results and competitive advantage—as CreAction does—finds acceptance in companies around the globe (eventually). Look at the Total Quality movement, for example.

But we shouldn't bet the ranch on this. Large companies are like huge ocean tankers. They don't change direction easily or quickly.

Religious/social ventures

Except when it comes to human rights and social justice, we shouldn't expect our religious institutions to play a lead role. It's not in their nature. Social ventures are another matter. Social entrepreneurial ventures are sprouting up all over the place because of deep societal needs. The principles in this book fit perfectly.

Start with your means. Take low-cost actions. Involve anyone who cares. Here, CreAction is a much better fit than classic business reasoning. The directors of these social ventures should take notice and stop requiring the overuse of formal planning, which everyone knows is foolish but won't say so. The directors need to release their social entrepreneurs from the shackles of exclusive use of Prediction and instead learn how to better support them.

Schools

This leaves our educational institutions. Their job is to teach thinking. And the CreAction we are advocating is easy to teach, because people already know it. They really only need to practice more. And for that to happen, it only needs to be legitimized as a complement to the Prediction reasoning that pervades our educational system.

It really won't take much additional time, if any at all. Just the discernment that in any particular situation you may exhaust the power of Prediction, and when you do, it's time to employ CreAction.

This can begin in kindergarten and continue at the postgraduate level. Nearly every course could include a CreAction complement. Teaching it could be exciting and could reinvigorate tired teachers and school systems. This can lift up all the disciplines and unite them to provide our society with citizens capable of 21st-century jobs, because they are capable of 21st-century thinking.

Where we come out

So, our government can provide incentives and can remove barriers.

Businesses can experiment, prove the value, and compete.

Social entrepreneurs can build new agencies and establish communities of like-minded people.

But most important, we—as parents, teachers, and students—can reclaim our heritage as creators.

All we need is to want it. And to start with what we have at hand; take small steps; bring our friends along; and build off what we find.

Answers to some of the most challenging questions we get

People are naturally skeptical, and rightfully so. If you are going to become an advocate for CreAction, and we hope you are, you can expect pushback. For what it is worth, here is how we respond to the questions we get.

1. This whole thing sounds too simple.

We know you didn't mean that as a compliment, but we would like to say thank you anyway. Making this simple and easy to understand was our intent. At its most basic, CreAction, a method that we believe can augment the way you think now, is something that we all did before we were introduced to more formal ways of reasoning.

As an infant/toddler/preschooler, everything you confronted for the first time was an unknown. Because it was, you tried certain things. You cried. You tried to walk. You put your finger in a light socket. And as a result of your actions, certain things happened. Some good. (Walking.) Some bad. (That shocking light socket.) But that is how you dealt with what, for you at the time, was an unpredictable universe. You took small steps to learn about it.

This way of approaching life has become unfamiliar to us over time, because it has been replaced by the Prediction reasoning used to explain reading, writing, and arithmetic, and just about everything else. But, our natural way of learning—the approach we had as children—has remained within you. We just want to help bring it out.

2. What the heck do you guys know about life in the real world? Why should I believe that this is anything other than just another egghead theory?

You're right about our backgrounds (although each of us has had substantial profit and loss responsibility throughout our careers). But the last thing we hope you do is believe this. Belief will get you nowhere; only action will. Either this makes enough (common) sense for you to try it or it doesn't. Don't take our word for it. Take a small, smart step and see if it feels right to you. If it does, take another.

3. This whole thing can be reduced to "ready, aim, fire," can't it? Isn't that stupid on its face?

As we've said, the summary really is: aim, fire. There's not a lot of getting ready. At its heart, we are saying that when you are in a situation where you don't know what is going to happen next, and the cost of acting is low, then fire with what is at hand or can be assembled quickly.

As for "this is stupid," you won't know if it's stupid for you until you try it. Until then, all you have is the *thought* that this may be stupid. That sure won't take you anywhere. (By the way, this approach has been proven by smart, successful serial entrepreneurs. They don't think it's stupid. That's what intrigued us in the first place.)

4. Who the heck has time for taking steps down a road that may lead nowhere? I have a finite amount of time, resources, and energy, and I simply can't afford to waste them.

Agreed. But you really have only three options when faced with the unknown. 1) You can sit there forever thinking and conclude the situation is hopeless, or the problem is too big, so you do nothing. 2) You can do all that thinking, and when you are absolutely, positively, sure, you act . . . only to find out that a) you may not have been right, or b) while you were doing all that thinking, someone beat you to the solution. Or 3) you can do enough thinking to take a smart step toward a solution, one that won't cost you a lot if you are wrong (leaving you enough resources to try again).

5. Maybe, I will grant you, this could work for people thinking about starting a small business, but I need $500 million for the biotech company I want to start. How is this going to help me?

It's probably not, at least not beyond the early phases of your project, which, by the way, is where biotech entrepreneurs and others who need a lot of money use it. Clearly, you can use all the principles of affordable loss to help you determine if you are truly committed to starting your manufacturing facility, biotech lab, or whatever the venture is that will consume a lot of capital. And once you get your money, you will use CreAction in your product development to some degree.

But at some point, you are going to need to attract serious money to make it happen. And that will mean finding serious investors, investors who are going to rely on—and will want you to rely on—Prediction.

That's perfectly fine. Remember what we have said. CreAction—and "affordable loss" is part of CreAction—isn't designed to replace Prediction. There are still going to be places—such as raising huge amounts of capital—where Prediction, with its emphasis on future cash ows and return on investment, is going to be the way to go. This is one of those places, so predict away.

One more thing about this. Those investors you will be asking for huge bucks are going to be looking to your background to see if you have ever started something successfully. The fastest way to get a new venture up and going is by using CreAction. So, if you don't have a success under your belt, you may want to use CreAction to help you start one (or two), before you go searching for those big bucks.

6. This is never going to work in the big company where I work.

You may be right. But as veterans of working in and with big companies, we know this: They will commit to anything that will help them make more money legally. They are not going to reject it out of hand if there is a promise that it will make them more success-ful. (If they do, the idea has been presented badly.)

7. Have you met our mayor? Town council? Reverend? What do you mean it can work in all aspects of my life?

Until you act, all you have is your thoughts. If you think it can't work and you don't act, you will be left with the thought that it can't work, and that will be a self-fulfilling prophecy.

Our whole argument is that you need to act to create what you want. Once you have acted, you have evidence. The evidence may confirm that this approach may not work with your town coun-cil—you really won't be able to overcome the politics that will get in the way—and maybe it won't work with your clergyperson. But we have seen it work with governments and religious organiza-tions. The bottom line: Until you act, you will never know for sure.

8. Maybe all this could work in business, but you don't know my mother-in-law, wacky sister, or offbeat friends. How can you possibly think this will work with families and friends?

You're right. It probably won't work with in-laws. But that just proves one of the great conundrums of human existence, by show-ing that God is not altogether all-loving, now, is She?

But although the dynamics are different with family and friends— the affordable loss concept is far more important, for example—we have seen the concepts work . . . and even get people dates.

9. If this is such a good idea, how come it is not being taught in schools?

Our question exactly. Our schools are now training people who are going to be in the workforce in the year 2065. Who the heck can predict what they will need to know. Since they are going into the vast unknown, they should be armed with as many potentially help-ful tools as possible, and clearly CreAction can be one of them. Our schools really are the place to teach thinking. And the thinking we are advocating here is easy to teach, because people already know it. They really only need to practice more. And for that to happen it only needs to be legitimized as a complement to all the Prediction reasoning that pervades our educational system, both in content and the processes by which that content is taught and administered. It really won't take much additional time, if any at all. Just the discernment that in any situation you may exhaust the power of Prediction. And when you do, it's time to employ CreAction. This can begin in prekindergarten and continue at the postgraduate level.

10. How can you possibly believe this can change the world? The problems we face are too intense/immense.

They are. And Entrepreneurial Thought and Action is hardly the whole solution. But it's part. (The neglected and insufficiently applied part. After all, entrepreneurs have made some absolutely wonderful contributions to humankind through the literally millions of things they have brought into being.)

As for our belief that individuals can change the world, let us quote Robert F. Kennedy, someone who said it better than we could:

> Few will have the greatness to bend history itself, but each of us can work to change the small portion of events, and in the total of all those acts will be written the history of this generation. It is from numerous diverse acts of courage and belief that human history is shaped. Each time a man stands for an ideal, or acts to improve the lot of others, or strikes out against injustice, he sends forth a tiny ripple of hope, and crossing each other from a million different centers of energy and daring, those ripples build a current that can sweep down the mightiest of walls of oppression and resistance.

The beauty of Entrepreneurial Thought and Action is that it creates a defined logic or reasoning around this thing called CreAction, which otherwise looks like a black box. It allows people to make CreAction explicit and apply it in any area of their life. It just becomes ordinary.

That takes us full circle, of course. People are bound to read what we have to say and think, "but I knew that." That's our hope.

The one-minute CreAction seminar

1 | **Know what you want.**

2 | **Act quickly with the means at hand.**

3 | **Be alert and open to what is, and what you are getting.**
Make reality your friend and asset; build off what you find.

4 | **Take steps based on your means and what you can afford and want to pay to play.** It's not what you're going to do; it's what you are going to do next. Spread risk and acquire resources as you go along.

5 | **Bring other people with you.**

6 | **Remain flexible in what you want *and* how you do it** based on your most current insights, until you achieve your goal.

Acknowledgements

This isn't a traditional book, so it is not surprising that the acknowledgements won't be either. The book had its genesis in July 2008, when Len, who had been vice chairman and chief operating officer of Limited Brands, returned to Massachusetts to become president of Babson College. There he reconnected with Charlie, who had started three companies over the course of his career consulting to organizations.

Babson had been ranked number one in the world for entrepreneurship for as long as there had been rankings, but had not recently stopped to examine what that really meant. What was it that the school was really teaching and talking about?

The Babson community entered into a series of conversations that resulted in the articulation of Entrepreneurial Thought and Action (ET&A) as an umbrella concept for the school's work. Len and Charlie decided to attempt to develop one answer to the question of what ET&A was. And they thought the best way to learn something is to try to teach it.

So in February of 2009 they created a course, each iteration of which evolved around the feedback and experiences of people (entrepreneurs, aspiring entrepreneurs, social entrepreneurs, families, friends, supporters, bosses of entrepreneurs—ages 16 to 70+) who participated in essentially developing the theory and practice of ET&A.

In the truest sense, this book is a report of what we have learned from those 300 people, coupled with some extensive research and literature. We owe special thanks to these alumni and friends: Dick Balzer, Paul Bauer, Les Charm, Mike Chmura, Mary Jo Cook, Eliot Daley, Pete Dolan, Diane Fulman, Carol Hacker, Kerry Hamilton, Miriam Hawley, Sherry Immediato, Cheryl Kiser, Martin Krag, Kurt Malkoff, Amy Rosen, Julia Ross, Johann Sadock, Richard Voos, Joel Yanowitz, Carl Youngman, and Ken Zolot.

The ET&A ideas also have roots in cognitive science, philosophy, business history, and beyond. The website (ActionTrumpsEverything.com) will provide the citations for those of you who find that particularly useful.

We begin the book by citing the research of Saras Sarasvathy, whose research describes the thought and action processes of serial entrepreneurs. In the course of our work we ended up finding that there were a number of additional ideas that extended that model. Beyond our own experience, our sources for these are found in working papers and discussions with Babson faculty, David Galenson's *Old Masters and Young Geniuses*, Alison Gopnik's *The Philosophical Baby*, Lewis Hyde's *The Gift*, William Irvine's *On Desire*, Nancy Koehn's *Brand New*, Frank Knight's *Risk, Uncertainty and Profit*, and Herbert Simon's *The Sciences of the Artificial*, to name just a few.

The ideas presented in this book have stood up to academic scrutiny and have been tested and verified independently of each other—in some cases over many decades—but so far, they have not been put together as we have presented them to you except in our course. While there is no existing research on the entire model, people with lifetimes of entrepreneurial experience say this resonates with them. In keeping with the book's premise, that's good enough for now.

The authors are enormously grateful for the support, enthusiasm, and contributions given to us by our wives: Carolyn Kiefer, Phyllis Schlesinger, and Alison Davis Brown.

And our children Peter Brown, Shannon Brown, Megan Kiefer, Adam Payne, Becca Schlesinger Ferat, Katie Schlesinger, Emily Schlesinger, Nick Viscomi and Sam Viscomi, who have contributed to the manuscript and the course, and perhaps most importantly contributed through their lives as case studies of Entrepreneurial Thought **in** Action.

And for untold hours of work helping to develop and express the ideas in their present form: Shahid Ansari, Scott Aronow, Chuck Conn, Heidi Sparkes Guber, Heidi Neck, Stever Robbins, and Steve Tritman.

Finally, for helping us turn a manuscript into a finished book we would like to thank: Ann Crews, Kristen Palson, Rebecca Saraceno and Jeffrey L. Seglin.